21st-Century Violinists

Violinists

Volume 1

STRING LETTER PUBLISHING

Publisher: David A. Lusterman
Editor: Mary VanClay
Associate Editor: Jessamyn Reeves-Brown
Assistant Editor: Marsha Gonick
Designer: Ann Leonardi
Production Coordinator: Judy Zimola

Contributors: Todd Brewster, Edith Eisler, Timothy Pfaff, Stephanie von Buchau

Front cover: Midori, photo by Jack Mitchell.
Back cover: Corey Cerovsek, photo by J. Henry Fair; Midori, photo by Jack Mitchell;
Pamela Frank, photo by Tania Mara.

This book was produced by String Letter Publishing, Inc.
PO Box 767
San Anselmo, California 94979
(415) 485-6946
www.stringsmagazine.com

Library of Congress Cataloging-in-Publication Data

21st century violinists.
        p. cm.-- (Strings backstage)
    ISBN 1-890490-26-1
    1. Violinists–Interviews. I. Title: Twenty-first century violinists. II. Series.

ML398 .A12 1999
787.2'092'2–dc21
[B]

99-046730

STRING LETTER PUBLISHING

TABLE OF CONTENTS

INTRODUCTION

The violin is often called the most singing, the most intimate of all musical instruments. It holds a cherished place in many cultures the world over and has certainly inspired some of the greatest composers and performers in Western classical music. In this collection of interviews, from the pages of *Strings* Magazine, some of the most talented, influential, and vital violinists of our time explain what inspired them to become musicians, what the virtuoso's life is like, and how they express themselves on this beloved instrument.

If we could have gathered these famous players together in one room, we might have expected them to start talking shop—what do *you* do to warm up, have you recorded any Bach yet, what on earth do you do with those eighth notes in the first phrase of the Brahms D-Minor Sonata? Well, we couldn't get them all in one room at once (with their busy concert schedules, some of them hardly have time to see their families). But gathering their interviews into one book seemed like the next-best thing. Reading them as a collection, it's striking how often the same themes come up; find out how many of these soloists are increasingly drawn to chamber music, for example, and how many like to "practice" without even touching their instruments.

It's also interesting to see how public expectations and reactions have changed over the ten-year span of these interviews. When Nadja Salerno-Sonnenberg (page 80) appeared on an album cover in the early 1990s in a low-cut dress, with plenty of leg showing, she caused a minor furor. Since then, however, glamorous presentations of classical musicians have become commonplace. And back in 1989, when Nigel Kennedy (page 40) was espousing his love for jazz and rock as well as classical music, he was making a controversial statement—but today, such mainstream heroes as violinist Joshua Bell and cellist Yo-Yo Ma regularly experiment with everything from Baroque music to American folk fiddle–style arrangements.

The vagaries of a changing era aside, what this group of interviews most clearly reveals are the commonalities that amount to eternal truths in the musical world. For example, it pays to practice (at least mentally if not physically), it's hard to play well when jet-lagged, and—of course, most important of all—finding joy in the music, in expressing and communicating human emotion, is what kindles the passion that unites virtuosos with their audiences.

Mary VanClay
Editor

Maxim
Vengerov

The Russian violinist Maxim Vengerov came to international atten-tion in the summer of 1989, when, at 14, he gave a highly acclaimed recital at the Concertgebouw in Amsterdam. Concert dates followed, as did the first-prize award at the Carl Flesch International Violin Competition in 1990. He left the former USSR that same year for Tel Aviv, and he now lives in Amsterdam.

With an increasingly impressive recording career, Vengerov has entered the top rank of today's classical-music superstars. But he retains an astonishing level of availability to his adoring public, and lines outside his dressing room suggest a rock star more than a clas-sical instrumentalist. He is further famous for having taken years off the lives of his violin's insurance underwriters by making a com-mercial jumping out of an airplane with his priceless Strad. It will probably mark the end of his life in advertising, but his place on the concert circuit is as secure as anyone's. This interview was held dur-ing a performance tour in late 1995.

Maximum Talent

Timothy Pfaff

The Russians have come. A flood of major musicians from post-Soviet Russia has enriched concert life in the West immeasurably—and for-ever altered some Western misconceptions about that still foreign-seeming land. Arguably among the most startling revelations is that musicians of great consequence—violinist Maxim Vengerov among them—have come to us from, of all places, Siberia. To Western minds schooled during the Cold War, Siberia is not a place people come from. It's the icy purgatory where political undesirables were sent—where peo-ple disappeared before *disappear* became a transitive verb.

Photo by Thomas Müller

But when teenager Maxim Vengerov left his homeland, toting his student violin and a talent more fully formed than his bones, he became news for reasons beyond his being from Siberia—or, for that matter, his being a conspicuously precocious youngster. Even though the international concert scene was saturated with fresh-faced violin prodigies, when Vengerov hit it, the waters parted. There was noticeably little talk about his being a "prodigy" and, instead, awestruck reports of a major new talent with great artistic depth. Was it time to send people to Siberia again?

To hear Vengerov tell it, not only was he not in exile in his home-

land, he was at the center of a spiritually warm and artistically nurturing musical world. The son of an orchestral oboist, he grew up in the rehearsal room. "I lived there," he recalls. "That was my life." His mother was famous throughout Russia as the director of a children's choir. Its youngest member, Vengerov sang in it from the age of three. His grandmother, he recalls, was "a great singer who could not have a career because of the war." In all, he speculates, "My parents and grandparents invested in me the lives they could not have and the things they were not able to do. Anyway, that's what my grandmother says."

Maxim Vengerov, born in 1975, comes from a musical family in Siberia.

Among Vengerov's calling cards in the West was a Biddulph CD featuring the standard piano-accompanied violin showpieces, word of which coursed through the string world like a forest fire. Vengerov soon signed with Teldec, with whom he has recorded a compelling range of repertoire. One of them, taped when Vengerov was a hoary old 18, just happened to snag *Gramophone*'s 1994 Record of the Year award.

It couldn't have happened to a nicer record. Although Vengerov's discography and concert repertoire include the expected Mendelssohn and Bruch, Beethoven and Brahms, the music on the award-winning recording—the first violin concertos of Prokofiev and Shostakovich, with the London Symphony Orchestra conducted by Mstislav Rostropovich (Teldec 92256)—is as distinctive as its proponent. The Prokofiev, played at white heat for what turns out to be a blistering performance, is jaw-slackening proof of the young man's virtuosity. The Shostakovich, intermittently as technically demanding, reveals the wise old man in the young man's suit.

At some 40 minutes, the Shostakovich Violin Concerto No. 1 is as substantive as many of the composer's great symphonies, and it is in no respect a lesser achievement. As a violin concerto, it ranks with the best of its 20th-century counterparts (in themselves a series of towering masterpieces). The piece, which charts a harrowing and often bleak spiritual landscape, also functions as an impassioned outcry against political oppression and inhumanity in all its guises. Its long passacaglia is one of our day's noblest and most solemn hymns. There was reason to think that the piece, first performed in 1955, would never have an exponent to compare with its dedicatee, David Oistrakh, who shared the composer's experience of state oppression as well as his artistic vision. Then along came Maxim Vengerov.

In the reviews of the London concerts that immediately preceded Vengerov's recording, the British press was all but tongue-tied over the incandescence of his live performance. The violinist gave the critics a news handle—and something extramusical to write about—when he broke a string in the concerto's spitfire final movement (he provides his own account of the now-famous incident in the following interview). String breaking has, subsequently, become something of a trademark of the young man's high-intensity playing. Almost obligingly, he underwent the same horror during the opening performance of a subscription run of the Brahms Violin Concerto with the San Francisco Symphony, under Michael Tilson Thomas, last November, only days before the following conversation.

Outgoing, personable, and manifestly inclined to laugh (most often at himself), Vengerov gets a lock on an interviewer with his eyes in the same way he enthralls an audience with his violin. Like his playing, his speech is full of surprises—heavily accented, of course, yet startlingly idiomatic in his way with a new language, and frequently arresting both in content and expression.

When you broke a string in the first movement of the Brahms Concerto the other night, you seemed almost unfazed. Does this happen often?

Normally it happens in the Shostakovich [Violin Concerto No. 1]. I break lots of strings there. It's my most expensive concerto. When I played it in New York, I broke two strings in the first rehearsal. It happens quite often, especially when the strings get a little older. After two days they are already quite fragile. Maybe they break because of the intensity of my playing. It happens with all the violins, so it's my fault, absolutely. I can't fight it. It gets on your nerves, but you get used to it.

The incredible time it happened was when I was playing the Shostakovich with Rostropovich [conducting the London Symphony Orchestra] at Barbican Hall in London, before we made the recording. I had a really good time with the whole concerto, and together we had some really marvelous moments. I felt that my response with the audience was so great and deep that we had totally great communication.

At the end of the fourth movement there are a lot of tricky passages, with many ups and downs. If you miss something, you will never get back on track. Just in this moment I broke a string. I grabbed the concertmaster's violin and started singing instead of playing. It was the only way I could think of to continue—singing, whistling, whatever.

During the Brahms in San Francisco, I was actually quite upset. The

What he plays

Maxim Vengerov plays an Antonio Stradivari violin, the "Kiesewetter," probably named for the German violinist Christoph Gottfried Kiesewetter (1777–1827), according to instrument expert Charles Beare. Disputes about the instrument's date are fueled by the fact that the label has been altered, and the violin is a "twin" of the "Emiliani" of 1723, made of the same wood and with other characteristics that suggest it was made the same year. Owned by Clement Arrison of Mark IV Industry, it was loaned to Vengerov by arrangements made through the Stradivari Society of Chicago's Bein & Fushi, Inc.

Vengerov, who previously played the 1727 "Reynier" Stradivari, prizes the "Kiesewetter" for its depth of sound. "It has a wonderful, sweet tone and, overall, the range of sound I need. It is not the loudest violin, but I don't need that, and this is a powerful instrument. I find it unique in the sense that it has all the qualities I need."

Vengerov plays with a Sartory bow, which he describes as "not my last-destination bow. I'm not exactly sure what I need; my right hand is still developing."

Vengerov's propensity for breaking strings has not prevented him from sticking with the strings he is familiar with and loves. He uses E strings by Pirastro and Jargar; the remainder are by Thomastik.

Claus Thumser

string broke at a moment I wouldn't like it to happen. When I took the concertmaster's violin, I found that it had a funny shoulder rest. So then I took the second player's instrument—and it was totally the same.

At least you got your Stradivari back in time for the wonderful cadenza you wrote. I understand that that cadenza is already a few years old.

I wrote it in 1992, for my premiere of the concerto with the Berlin Philharmonic and [Claudio] Abbado. I had fun with it. I wanted to continue the tradition of the masters of the last century, when a violinist was obliged to write his own cadenza to express his feelings about the concerto. I love the Kreisler and Joachim candenzas, but I thought I had a few ideas of my own to express. I've written several cadenzas for a Mozart concerto, so I thought I could to it for the Brahms. For the Beethoven it is more interesting, because he already wrote one of his own. So, when I do that, I don't know whether I'm going to do a combination with that one or do something totally different.

That's impressive work for any violinist today, and the more so for someone your age. Did you study composition?

No. That's what I want to do next. I think it would be great for my growth. I want to know as much as possible about music, so I can express myself more fruitfully.

So how did you come to write cadenzas? The Brahms seemed very musical—and rather advanced.

Part of the reason I have so many ideas is that I have met so many great people during the time I have been studying this concerto. I have passed through many stages with it. Once I came to [Daniel] Barenboim, and he turned everything upside down, completely. It was a shock to me.

I have two musical fathers, Rostropovich and Barenboim, and every time I come to them, I no longer realize where the ground is, and where the sky. Thanks to them, I see no limitations in music making.

What do you mean by that, exactly?

When I came to Rostropovich with the Shostakovich, he turned my mind about music in general as well as about the concerto. Of course he gave me a lot of great ideas for the Prokofiev and the Shostakovich, but more than that, we talked about music. He encouraged me to look at the music much more deeply, not only in a horizontal way but also vertical. Our problem as instrumentalists is that we have only one line. But it is important to look at a concerto in complex, to see your instrument as one part in the whole system. It's great being part of the whole and not just the soloist. Since I left my last violin teacher, I have been developing in a different way: not just as a virtuoso in instrumental matters but as a musical virtuoso.

And with Barenboim I can no longer be just a violinist. He tries to take me away from the instrument, which gives me great satisfaction afterwards. It's like when he plays the piano: you hear all the voices, a whole orchestra. I'll never forget hearing him play the Beethoven "Appassionata" in Paris. He played it like a big symphony; it was just astonishing. His playing helped me understand the idea of instrumental colors.

What I mean when I say that Barenboim takes me away from my instrument is that when I am making music with him, I don't depend anymore on the violin. Music doesn't depend on the instrument; the instrument depends on the music. The music is the important thing; the violin is just here to do it, to express it. You could express the same idea in different ways. The violin just gives one path to your interpretation. And although they are completely different, Rostropovich and Barenboim share this view. That is why it is a great joy to work with them.

Chris Lee

Vengerov playing with the New York Philharmonic under Kurt Masur in 1997.

What do you look for in a conductor?

I appreciate it when a conductor gives me his long-term experience with the music—even if he doesn't exactly say anything about it. Sometimes it takes me a long time to understand all their ideas. For example, I met Rostropovich one and a half years ago [in late 1994], and I am only beginning to grasp some of the things he has taught me about the Shostakovich. With him I sometimes have to be much older than I am—sometimes a half-century older. It can be very frightening.

My first experience of this kind was when I first met Barenboim, four years ago. I had played an audition for him—the Bach Chaconne and the Tchaikovsky Concerto—the previous year, and he was excited and invited me to play in Chicago, the Sibelius Concerto. When I arrived for the piano rehearsal, I had just played the concerto in a BBC Promenade concert in London, and I was kind of proud of myself that I knew the concerto technically and musically—I thought. So I played through the whole concerto with Barenboim, and when I finished his face was so pale, you know? After a few minutes' silence, I said, "Maestro, can you tell me something?" He said, "I don't know what to say. I think you can't afford to be playing like this." Can you imagine for me, as a young guy, hearing that? He continued, "I thought you really were a good musician, and I had hopes for you, that you could approach music in an essential way. You are playing wonderfully; your technique is perfect—but this is not Sibelius. There is no personal touch, none of your own personal approach to it."

For me, it was like going from childhood to hearing someone talk philosophy. I asked him, "Could you tell me how to approach it?" He said, "Of course I could, but I think you should find out for yourself."

I thought I knew this concerto as well as I could, but he directed me to a few places in it—in order that I could find my own way in it, not just [the way] it comes to the fingers.

I had only one night to think it over, and I spent that night with the score. I left the violin on the table, because it was no longer necessary. At first it was like looking at the empty ceiling; I didn't see anything but notes. Then, from the way it goes in the score, I started to realize fantastic things, and I discovered my own interpretation. By the next morning I had a totally different approach to the music. When I went to thank Barenboim, he said, "You did it for yourself."

I love the way he looks at me when he conducts. Last year we played four concerts together. I often see him looking at me, wanting to say something, but when I ask him, he says, "No, I save it for later. You're not ready for that." Then, when I ask him about it at the next concert, he says, "You know? You already did it." I love that kind of internal communication with the people with whom I make music.

Has your new attitude toward the violin affected your practice regime?

I used to put in a lot of hours practicing. Now I'm perhaps at the other extreme: I don't practice at all, or I try as much as possible to get away from it. There has been enough of manual practice. Sometimes it is not necessary and spoils your playing. When you play a phrase over and over, you lose the will to improvise, to approach it in another way. I try never to repeat even one phrase the same.

Have you been influenced by the thinking of the historical-performance practitioners? For example, have you consulted the first edition of the Brahms Concerto score?

Yes, and I follow very much the [Nikolaus] Harnoncourt approach to music. I admire him and his intelligence, and his will to approach music in an essential way—to be as close to the composer as possible. In the beginning I try to follow the composer's will, to discover the way he wanted me, the performer, to play his music. I try to get as much as I can from the score, and every time I look at a score, I learn something more. You can never be better than the composer. But a score is like an abbreviation—like initials. We have to get to know what the meaning of them is. We performers are the ones who have to make it work.

Have original-instrument performers influenced the way you play, say, Bach?

Yes. I try to follow what they do, because I think there are many inklings in it. I think it would help me even more to work with conductors of this kind, and work with them directly. I can read books

Recordings

Beethoven: Sonata No. 9 ("Kreutzer"); Brahms: Sonata No. 2 in A Major. With Alexander Markovich, piano (Teldec 74001).

Beethoven: Sonata No. 5; Mozart: Sonata in B-flat Major; Mendelssohn: Sonata in F Major. With Itamar Golan, Alexander Markovich, piano (Teldec 76349).

Brahms: Concerto; Sonata No. 3. With the Chicago Symphony, Daniel Barenboim, cond. and piano (Teldec 17144).

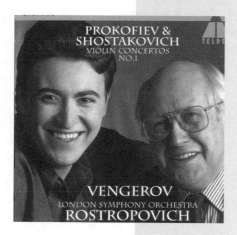

Bruch: Concerto No. 1 in G Minor; Mendelssohn: Concerto in E Minor. Gewandhausorchester Leipzig, Kurt Masur, cond. (Teldec 90875).

Paganini: Concerto No. 1; Waxman: Carmen Fantasie; Saint-Saëns: Havanaise, Introduction and Rondo Capriccioso. Israel Philharmonic Orchestra, Zubin Mehta, cond. (Teldec 73266).

Prokofiev: Concerto No. 1; Shostakovich: Concerto No. 1. London Symphony Orchestra, Mstislav Rostropovich, cond. (Teldec 92256).

Prokofiev: Concerto No. 2; Shostakovich: Concerto No. 2. London Symphony Orchestra, Mstislav Rostropovich, cond. (Teldec 13150).

The Road I Travel: Music of Tchaikovsky, Waxman, Brahms, Mozart, Mendelssohn, Beethoven, Massenet, Shostakovich (Teldec 17045).

Sibelius: Concerto in D Minor; Nielsen: Concerto, Op. 33. Chicago Symphony Orchestra, Daniel Barenboim, cond. (Teldec 13161).

Tchaikovsky: Concerto in D Major; Glazunov: Concerto in A Minor. Berlin Philharmonic, Claudio Abbado, cond. (Teldec 90881).

Virtuoso Vengerov: Music of Paganini, Sarasate, Kreisler, Wieniawski, Tchaikovsky, Bazzini, Messiaen, Bloch. With Ita Margolin, piano (Teldec 77351).

about it, but I would like to work more directly with other musicians who play with this historical understanding. I think their work is quite revolutionary.

But from the first I heard his music I have never moved away from Bach. I think Bach and Monteverdi are the basis of all that we do as musicians. Every day I play Bach.

Your recording activity suggests that you are moving toward more contemporary music. Is this so?

Yes. I couldn't have predicted it two years ago, but I am going from the Classical-Romantic repertoire to the contemporary works now. It was with my association with Rostropovich that I started to play Prokofiev, and now I am moving toward Stravinsky and [Alfred] Schnittke. Actually, I have played a lot of contemporary Russian music. When I was studying, I don't think I missed any of the Soviet music for violin.

One of the pieces I first learned when I was ten—[Rodion] Shchedrin's "Echo" Sonata—I am playing on my recital tour this spring. Of all the Soviet composers, Shchedrin was the tough cookie to study, but I think this is a really great work. He dedicated it to Bach, and it is full of quotations from the Bach sonatas and partitas. That is where he gets the idea of the echo. The piece is interesting and also entertaining. I think it is a great joy for the public.

How important are recitals and chamber music to your life as a performer?

I have played as a member of string trios, piano trios, quartets, and quintets. Actually, I would love to establish my own piano trio or string quartet, but I need to find the right cellist. Playing this material is very different from playing concertos, but I think, in the long term, I prefer it. With it I can express myself fully.

Chamber and recital music is one of the most important aspects of my life. I could never do without it. The best repertoire—the greatest music—is chamber music. It is the soul of music. Most of what the public knows of this aspect of my playing is from my recitals with Ito Margolin, who teaches at the Paris Conservatoire and also is my pianist, including on the records. I feel a special communication with him. When he and I can deliver messages from the composers, communicate with each other, and communicate—really make contact with—the audience, that means there are quite a lot of personalities involved. It is the most naked kind of music making, the most exposed. And for me it is the most exciting.

Anne-Sophie
Mutter

In the more than two decades since conductor Herbert von
Karajan launched her career, Anne-Sophie Mutter has become one
of the most acclaimed violinists of her generation. She performs as
a soloist and chamber musician, has an award-winning discography, and has established the Anne-Sophie Mutter Foundation to
support talented young string players worldwide.

The following interview took place in the summer of 1992.
Since then, Mutter has had a second child. She has also unfortunately been widowed. However, she has carried on her career with
award-winning recordings and concert tours. She continues to
explore the classical repertoire (she staged a global tour in 1998
with pianist Lambert Orkis, playing the ten Beethoven sonatas),
and she has increasingly become known as a master interpreter of
contemporary music. "Without it," she said in 1997, "my life
would be much poorer. It has enriched my technique, deepened my
understanding of orchestral scores, and, I think, made me a more
interesting musician." With a deep commitment to expanding the
violin's repertoire, she has worked with some of today's best-
known composers, including Sebastian Currier, Norbert Moret,
Witold Lutoslawski, and Krzysztof Penderecki.

The Natural

Edith Eisler

There are performers who have such a natural gift for their instrument that it seems to be an extension of their body. Their playing
gives the impression of a consummate ease and relaxation that has led
audiences, as well as great teachers accustomed to working with the
best talents, to regard them as favorites of the gods.

One of these is violinist Anne-Sophie Mutter. She burst upon the musical scene in 1976 at the age of 13 with a recital in Lucerne, which created such a stir that it came to the attention of Herbert von Karajan, then music director of the Berlin Philharmonic. He invited her to audition for him and engaged her as his soloist for several concerts and a series of recordings, which effectively started her on an international career.

If this sounds like the typical launching of a child prodigy, that is not the way Mutter describes her violinistic beginnings.

"To create a prodigy, there has to be a teacher or a mother with a whip, so to speak, and mine were not like that at all," she says. "Besides, it wouldn't have worked—I was too stubborn. I grew up in the Black Forest, in a very calm, nice little village. My parents were not musicians, but we listened to a lot of recordings, and when I was about five, I suddenly decided I wanted to be a violinist. Don't ask me why—I must have heard some violin music that I liked.

"So I started piano lessons at five and a half, but thank God I convinced my parents after a few months that it was the violin I really wanted to play. My first teacher was Erna Honigberger, who

Even as an eight-year-old, Mutter played seriously.

had been a pupil of Carl Flesch. She was half Jewish and had come to our little village from Berlin because of the war. As a concert artist, she called herself Erna Mottl, because she also played in coffee houses and probably did not want to be recognized, so she had taken the name from the conductor Felix Mottl. She was wonderful, especially with small children; I still remember her way of teaching vividly. She had a lot of patience and the ability never to let her students feel they were learning something. Working with her was very relaxed, full of joy, and things sort of happened naturally. I went to her every morning, five days a week. First we sat down and had breakfast, although I'd already had one at home, and then we started to work a little bit—at least that's how it seemed. She had turtles and dogs in her living room; it was really chaotic. She was just great.

"After half a year, when I was six, I took part in the biggest German competition for youngsters, where I won the first prize, with a special commendation which has never been given to anybody before or since. I played a caprice by Federigo Fiorillo and a sonata by Handel."

Mutter must have been a very serious little violinist even then; a photograph of her playing at about eight years of age already shows the same frown of concentration she still wears when she performs.

Since most of her day was taken up with the violin, she studied privately instead of attending school. "I had to take an examination twice a year, to show that I had covered all the subjects in the curriculum, and, until I was 14, I also had to play for the school authorities once a year, to prove that I deserved this special treatment; but when Karajan began to take an interest in me, they finally believed it. I graduated when I was 18.

"Unfortunately, Erna Honigberger died after I had studied with her for four years. At that point, my parents told me that if I wanted to stop, this would be the time to do it, because there were no teachers around our little town and it was very difficult to find somebody who would teach the same method. I did not want to change my technique, my way of holding the violin, because it all worked very well. And of course I didn't want to stop, so I was without a teacher for nine months.

"During that time, I prepared on my own for another level of the same competition, which wasn't too bad for a ten-year-old. And I won the first prize with distinction again, with Tartini's 'Devil's Trill' Sonata, Bach's Chaconne, and Sarasate's *Zigeunerweisen*. What's more, many of my much older fellow students asked me for advice with their violinistic problems. After that, I went to Geneva to play for Henryk Szeryng and asked him to recommend a teacher. He suggested Aida Stucki; they had both been students of Carl

Mutter developed a large repertoire of major works early in her career.

Flesch in Lucerne during his last years, and they were good friends. She was a wonderful violinist. I went to her twice a week for very long lessons, and it was with her that I really started working on style, not just on playing the violin. She lived in Switzerland, not very far from us, maybe an hour by train or an hour and a half by car. She became not only my main teacher, but my best friend. I've known her for 19 years now.

"At 13, I started to concertize. My first recital at the Lucerne International Music Festival had quite an interesting program with a bit of everything on it: the Bach Chaconne, Paganini's Caprice No. 24, the 'Devil's Trill' Sonata, *Zigeunerweisen,* and some Kreisler pieces. Karajan heard about it and invited me to Berlin to play for him at a rehearsal of the Philharmonic Orchestra, while the players were sitting in the auditorium, listening. My first concert with him was in 1977, in Salzburg, in Mozart's G-Major Concerto. And then things began to happen very quickly: we recorded the Mozart, and after that the concertos of Beethoven, Brahms, Mendelssohn, Bruch, and then *The Four Seasons* of Vivaldi . . . "

I remark that this must have meant learning all these major works very young and very fast. "It sounds that way," she answers, "but really I had plenty of time to grow naturally and started concertizing very gradually. From my sixth to my 13th year, I gave only two recitals a season. I first played with an orchestra when I was nine, in the Mozart

What she plays

Anne-Sophie Mutter's violin is an Antonio Stradivari made in 1710, the "Lord Dunraven," which she got in about 1983; she also has a Stradivari made in 1703, the "Emiliani." Talking about the instruments brings up a subject I had originally intended to avoid. "You play in these off-the-shoulder dresses," I ask. "What happens to the violin on the bare skin?"

From the quizzical expression on her face at the mention of her décolletage, I can tell that she had expected a different question, and she now breaks into a wide grin. "Nothing; I don't perspire much, and certainly not on the shoulder. But on the left side of the violin, where the hand goes up and down, and perspiration accumulates and damages the violin, I do have a piece of plastic to protect the original varnish. It's very easy to put on and take off. Don't worry, I take good care of my violin!"

I say that most people at least fold a handkerchief over the chin rest. "But that gets slippery, and also you have something between you and the violin. When you haven't, the instrument sort of gets glued to the skin; that's what makes it so great," she says.

"Have you always played without a pad or shoulder rest?"

"No, I started with a very high one, called the Menuhin, and it just did not work. When I was eight or nine, I played Sarasate's Zigeunerweisen a lot. Of course, I didn't have a lot of technical proficiency yet, and I pushed my shoulder up, so whenever I started that piece," she sings and demonstrates the beginning, attacking an imaginary violin, "I dug into it so hard that the shoulder rest just broke and hung down all the way through the piece. When I went to Aida Stucki, she tried to have me use a pad instead, but that didn't work either. From a pad, we went down to a little plastic thing that looked like the head of a meat hammer, with those notches—"

"Notches!" I exclaim. "That must have been terribly painful!"

She nods. "Yes, it hurt, it was awful, but it wasn't slippery, and it had a good height. But of course it didn't last long, and when I played with Karajan, I used only a thin piece of chamois, which I stuck to the edges of the violin with a little Scotch tape. And then one day, I got very adventurous and took it off," she makes a triumphant gesture, "because I was fed up with all that taping, and I played with nothing. You can see that my neck is very short and that the violin fits perfectly if I just turn my head slightly to the left; I don't have to push or squeeze. I find having anything under the violin really very uncomfortable.

"Another thing that's very important for me is having the chin rest in the middle, over the tailpiece, instead of on the left side. I think that was originally Carl Flesch's idea. It completely changes the position, because you don't have to turn the head so far to the left. And the violin is placed more on the shoulder, so it doesn't slide down the chest at a slant. That's much better for one's posture; I would recommend it to orchestra players and anybody who has back problems."

Concerto, K. 211; I learned the Mendelssohn Concerto when I was 11, and I remember I found the slow movement boring, because I was too young to understand it. I played Mozart, Bruch, and Mendelssohn with Karajan when I was 13, and he worked with me on the Beethoven very carefully for two years, making me listen to the orchestra, think about creating long lines. . . . He was fanatic about that and plagued not only me, but the orchestra, about imperceptible bow changes. We recorded it when I was 15. I did not study too many concertos until I was 18 or 19. There was one—I'd rather not name it—that I did learn too early and have never been able to make peace with. That's why I believe it's important to develop slowly, so the head will keep pace with the fingers. Aida Stucki was very careful not to let me play anything that was beyond me; she felt as responsible for all my performances as if they had been her own."

Mutter first came to America in 1980 on the crest of her European success, but her advance publicity seemed to focus more on her glamorous appearance, her striking good looks and designer evening gowns, than on her playing. It reminded me of the public's reaction to certain actresses who are so beautiful that people overlook how well they act. Sheila Porter, who became Mutter's publicist in 1986, says, "Truly glamorous violinists don't come along very often. But Anne-Sophie knows exactly what she wants; she's not going to change the way she lives, or the way she dresses, even if people talk about it. She wears those gowns on stage because she finds them comfortable to play in." In fact, Mutter says that the purpose of the off-the-shoulder style of her dresses is to permit immediate contact with the violin.

Mutter with conductor Herbert von Karajan, who helped launch her career.

I first heard Mutter at her Carnegie Hall debut recital in 1988. While all the violinistic expectations aroused by what I had been reading and hearing about her were amply fulfilled, there were also a few surprises. Watching her on stage was a pleasure because she did nothing to call attention to herself and seemed to take her genuine beauty completely for granted. Even the famous gowns, though they made the most of her figure, turned out to be elegant without being showy, and in the best of taste. She behaved with restraint and dignity, standing almost perfectly still, and projected an unaffected modesty and charm. Her tone had an incredible beauty and purity and appeared to flow naturally from her to the instrument, making the assertion that she wants the violin to rest directly on her skin entirely believable. Here, I thought, is the sort of radiant talent reserved for a chosen few.

She was very young at the time, and I felt that her technical virtuosity was ahead of her musical maturity, but when I heard her again a few years later, she seemed to have reached a new depth of inner concentration. By then she also become involved in playing contemporary music, for which she has developed a special affinity. In the summer of 1992, she made her concerto debut at a number of festivals: with the Mostly Mozart Orchestra in New York, the Boston Symphony at Tanglewood, and the Chicago Symphony at Ravinia, with whom she premiered and recorded *Time Chant* by Wolfgang Rihm and also played and recorded the Alban Berg Concerto, with James Levine conducting.

On the day of her Mostly Mozart appearance, I visit her at the small, elegant, European-style hotel where she always stays in New York. On being warned that her time will be very limited, since she has a rehearsal immediately afterward, I express concern that my visit will give her no chance to eat lunch, and am told that she never does. When I arrive, I find another interviewer about to leave, although it is only the middle of the morning. Clearly, her life is organized with the utmost efficiency, and when I watch her play later that evening, I realized that this also applies to her violin technique: she wastes no energy on unnecessary movements, her fingers stay close to the strings, her bow change is barely perceptible, and she avoids extraneous body motions.

Mutter has focused increasingly on contemporary music.

Seeing Mutter in an informal setting, casually dressed, confirms that hers is the kind of beauty not in need of glamorous gowns. She is in complete command of herself and the situation, and she radiates charm, youthful vivacity, and an endearing blend of self-confidence and modesty. I offer her the choice of speaking German, our shared native tongue, but she has already had an interview in English that morning and decides to stay on the same track. Her English is excellent; she says she learned it in school and by traveling.

After talk about her early training and career, I ask when and how she began to play so much modern music.

"I had my first contact with real contemporary music in 1986. [The Swiss conductor] Paul Sacher asked me if I wanted to give the premiere of Witold Lutoslawski's *Chain 2*. Soon after that, Lutoslawski orchestrated his Partita for me, and then came Norbert Moret's *En Rêve*. I have also recorded all of these for Deutsche Grammophon. I premiere a major new work about every other year. This year it was Wolfgang Rihm's *Time Chant*. Next year, it will be a new concerto by Krzysztof Penderecki. I am interested in studying pieces that will stay in my repertoire and that will also broaden and enrich the literature in general."

When I say that I was greatly impressed with her playing of *Chain 2,* together with the Bruch Concerto, with the New York Philharmonic, her self-possession melts into a radiant smile. Had all the new works been written for her or commissioned by her?

"No, they were all commissioned for me by Paul Sacher, except the Penderecki piece, which was commissioned by the Leipzig Rundfunk Orchestra. Most of them are dedicated to me."

"Suppose you find that you don't like one—would you still have to play it?"

"Yes, I think I would, but that hasn't happened yet. You know, as a musician, you identify so strongly with whatever piece of music you have in front of you that you want to make something out of it."

"But since you have to take it as it comes . . . "

She bursts out laughing. "Don't ask that question, it makes me nervous! I haven't seen the Penderecki yet."

"I know the Viola Concerto, which is very good, so why shouldn't the Violin Concerto be just as good? Besides, these are all composers of substance."

"Yes, but some change their style quite a lot. Penderecki certainly has, so I don't know what to expect. But I'm looking forward to seeing his piece. As for Lutoslawski, I had an immediate intellectual and emotional connection with his work from the very beginning."

I say that I had felt that she played his music as if she owned it, with total identification, and again her face lights up. How long does it take to learn a piece like that? She sighs. "Nobody asks me how long it takes, they just deliver the music a few weeks before the premiere and leave me to deal with it. I got the Rihm at the beginning of May and the premiere was in June; it was the same with the Lutoslawski."

"Since you know all these composers, can you ask them to make changes, if necessary?"

"Yes, but I never want to change any notes, only dynamics and tempo."

"Nothing violinistic?"

"No, I am much too proud to tell them that anything is too difficult; I just go ahead and learn it." I try to make it clear that I was not thinking of making the music easier, only of helping it to sound better, because composers often don't know enough about the violin. She agrees. "Most of them don't, but that's my problem. I think it is essential for a composer to have the freedom to write music as he imagines it, from his own standpoint, not that of the violinist. If you see a phrase that's not well written and you know what the composer wants to express, it's up to you to bring it out. There are a lot of things you can do to make a piece sound better without changing it. That's why dynamics are so important, especially if you also adjust the orchestration." Suddenly she laughs. "Penderecki frightened me a little by saying he might write a piece even more difficult than the one he wrote for Isaac Stern, so I may have to give in and ask him to make a few changes."

Recordings

Bartók: Concerto No. 2; Moret: En Rêve. Boston Symphony Orchestra, Seiji Ozawa, cond. (Deutsche Grammophon 431 626).

Beethoven: Triple Concerto, Op. 56; Overtures: Fidelio, Egmont, Coriolan. With Mark Zeltser, piano; Yo-Yo Ma, cello; Berlin Philharmonic, Herbert von Karajan, cond. (DG 415 276).

Beethoven: Concerto. Berlin Philharmonic, Herbert von Karajan, cond. (DG 413 818).

Beethoven: The String Trios, Opp. 3, 8; Op. 9, Nos. 1–3. With Bruno Giuranna, viola; Mstislav Rostropovich, cello (DG 427 687).

Beethoven: Complete Sonatas for Piano and Violin. With Lambert Orkis, piano (DG 457 619).

Berg: Concerto; Rihm: Gesungene Zeit. Chicago Symphony Orchestra, James Levine, cond. (DG 437 093).

The Berlin Recital: Works by Mozart, Brahms, Franck, Debussy. With Lambert Orkis, piano (DG 445 826).

Brahms: Concerto; Mendelssohn: Concerto. Berlin Philharmonic, Herbert von Karajan, cond. (DG 445 515).

Brahms: Concertos. With Maurizio Pollini, piano; António Meneses, cello; various conductors (DG 449 607).

Brahms: Concerto; Schumann: Fantasie. New York Philharmonic Orchestra, Kurt Masur, cond. (DG 457 075).

Brahms: Violin Concerto and Double Concerto, with António Meneses, cello; Berlin Pilharmonic with Herbert von Karajan, cond. (DG 439 007).

Bruch: Concerto No. 1; Mendelssohn: Concerto. Berlin Philharmonic, Herbert von Karajan, cond. (DG 400 031).

Carmen Fantasy: Works by Ravel, Sarasate, Massenet, Fauré, Tartini, Wieniawski. Vienna Philharmonic, James Levine, cond. (DG 437 544).

The Great Violin Concertos: Works by Mozart, Beethoven, Mendelssohn, Bruch, Brahms. Berlin Philharmonic, Herbert von Karajan, cond. (DG 415 565).

Lalo: Symphonie espagnole, Op. 21; Sarasate: Zigeunerweisen, Op. 20; Georges Bizet, Carmen Suite Nos. 1–2, Jeux d`enfants, Op. 22. Orchestre National de France, Seiji Ozawa, cond. (EMI Classics 5 69861 2 1).

Lutoslawski: Partita for Violin and Orchestra, Chain 2, Chain 3, Novelette. With Phillip Moll, piano. BBC Symphony Orchestra, Witold Lutoslawski, cond. (DG 445 576; with Stravinsky Violin Concerto, DG 423 696).

Meditation: Works by Vivaldi, Mozart, Massenet, Sarasate. Various orchestras and conductors (EMI 5 55266 2 5).

Mozart: Concerto No. 1, Sinfonia concertante and Adagio. With Bruno Giuranna, viola; Academy of St. Martin in the Fields, Sir Neville Marriner, cond. (EMI 7 54302 2).

Mozart: Concertos Nos. 2, 4. Philharmonia Orchestra London, Riccardo Muti, cond. (EMI 5 69865 2 7).

Mozart: Concertos Nos. 3, 5. Berlin Philharmonic, Herbert von Karajan, cond. (DG 415 327).

Mozart: Concerto in A Major; Bruch: Concerto in G Minor; Sarasate: Carmen Fantasie. Berlin Philharmonic, Herbert von Karajan, cond.; Vienna Philharmonic, James Levine, cond. (DG 459 042).

Mozart: Concerto No. 1; Bach: Concerto in E Major; Massenet: Meditation from "Thaïs"; Sarasate: Zigeunerweisen, Op. 20. Various orchestras and conductors (EMI 4 78365 2 7).

Mutter Modern: Music by Lutoslawski, Stravinsky, Bartók, Moret, Berg, Rihm. Various orchestras and conductors (DG 445 487).

Mutter/Rostropovich (Prokofiev: Concerto No. 1; Glazunov: Concerto, Op. 82; Chedrin: Stihara). Mstislav Rostropovich, cond. (Erato 0630-17722).

Penderecki: Metamorphosen; Bartók: Sonata for Violin and Piano No. 2. With Lambert Orkis, piano; London Symphony Orchestra, Krzysztof Penderecki, cond. (DG 453 507).

Romance: Music of Wieniawski, Bruch, Tchaikovsky, Mendelssohn, Brahms, and others. Berlin Philharmonic, Herbert von Karajan, cond.; Vienna Philharmonic, James Levine, cond. (DG 447 070).

Sibelius: Concerto; Serenades, Op. 69; Humoresque, Op. 87, No. 1. Staatskapelle Dresden, André Previn, cond. (DG 447 895).

Tchaikovsky: Concerto. Vienna Philharmonic, Herbert von Karajan, cond. (DG 419 241).

Vivaldi: The Four Seasons; Tartini: Devil's Trill. Vienna Philharmonic, Herbert von Karajan, cond. (1984, on EMI 7 47043 2). With the Trondheim Soloists (1999, on DG 289 463259).

"Do you feel that you have more affinity for some modern composers than others?"

"Not necessarily. There are some pieces I don't like, and I don't play them." Prompted to be more specific, she smiles. "The Schoenberg Concerto, for example; I really don't feel anything for it, but maybe that will change in time. I had a lot of problems with the Berg Concerto ten or 15 years ago, but now I've come to understand what a deep, tragic work it is."

Mutter feels that in Europe, audiences respond more positively to contemporary music than in America, because they have closer contact with it. "You need constant exposure, because you cannot really enjoy and learn to love modern music until your ear starts to adapt and understand what it hears. On the other hand, my audience at Tanglewood, where I played Mozart's A-Major Concerto a couple of days ago, really touched me—they were so incredibly quiet! It was outdoors, and it was raining terribly, too." I say that I thought the huge Tanglewood shed was the wrong place for Mozart, but she disagrees vigorously. "No, it's wonderful! Roger Norrington [the English conductor and performance-practice expert who substituted for the ailing Seiji Ozawa] made it so transparent, so vivid and alive. We did it with a reduced orchestra, and it worked very well. I love playing outdoors, where one can reach 5,000 people. And anyway, my theory is that you don't have to play loudly to be heard. It's a question of how you project, and Seiji, who came to the concert, told me he heard everything, although he was sitting all the way in the back."

She will be playing the same concerto at the New York Mostly Mozart Festival that evening and I ask how she adjusts to the differences between various orchestras, especially within two days. "Yes, that is quite difficult, but it's just one of the problems in a musician's life. We all have a certain interpretation in our ear, but you don't want to keep repeating yourself like a parrot, so you try to remain open and objective. You also have to take an orchestra's and a conductor's ability and character into consideration, so it is always different, wherever you play. Nevertheless, in the rehearsals you must, in a very short time, try to achieve whatever you think you can take responsibility for."

I ask how many rehearsals she gets with an orchestra and whether she has any contact with the conductor before the rehearsals start.

"Basically two, sometimes three rehearsals. For the Berg Concerto and the Rihm piece, I think we had four, so it depends on the program. I always have a rehearsal with the conductor beforehand, with or without piano, so we know exactly what we want before we go on stage with the orchestra. Otherwise you waste too much time."

We discuss cadenzas for the Mozart concertos. For the A Major, she is using Joachim's. "The one in the second movement I think is pretty strange, so I cut it a good deal; the one for the first movement is all right, and those in the last movement are just transitions—they are very nice. Joachim also wrote cadenzas for the D-Major Concerto, No. 4, but not for the G Major, No. 3. For that, there is a very good one by Sam Franko. The First and Second Concertos, K. 207 and 211, are a problem; I made my own cadenzas for those, grabbed a few things from here and there and mixed them together until they made sense."

"Do you play that D-Major Concerto that is called No. 7? They say it's not authentic Mozart, but it's very beautiful."

"Is that K. 271-A? Yes, I used to play it quite a lot; I even auditioned for Karajan with the first and second movements. It's very nice, but when all the discussion started about whether it was really by Mozart or maybe by Enesco, I stopped playing it."

Regarding her basic repertoire, she says, "I avoid works which are not really interesting for me to play, like—I don't know, Wieniawski, Vieuxtemps."

"What about Sarasate? I heard you play the *Carmen Fantasie* with so much fire and abandon."

"Sarasate is fun, if you have a balanced repertoire; he has style and is not too . . . perfumed," she laughs. She has recorded and played most of the great concertos.

I remark that I've always admired her bow control and have frequently noticed not only that

Early on, Mutter gained the admiration of her colleagues as well as her audience.

her bow change is imperceptible to both ear and eye, but that, even when she seems to have come to the very end of the frog, she still has room to spare. "It's mostly a matter of will power," she responds. "You have to plan ahead very carefully to make sure you'll have enough space at the heaviest part of the bow, where you need it most. Also, I keep my right arm fairly high and I think it gives me a feeling of control, of being on top of things."

Her recital programs vary from year to year. "The Schubert *Fantasie* I played last year is quite a piece—very rarely recorded, very rarely played; it's extremely difficult, for both players, technically, and also in terms of content. Looking into a lot of Schubert's *Lieder* helped; the variation movement is based on one: 'Sei mir gegrüsst.' It's very brilliant, but it must not sound like an express train or it becomes a showpiece."

She has two pianists who tour with her regularly: Lambert Orkis, who plays with her in America, and Philip Moll, who accompanies her in Europe and also sometimes in America.

Although she used to play string trios and piano trios, she does not perform chamber music at the moment because "it is just too difficult to get more than two people on the stage together. Recitals are more realistic. We rehearse anywhere, in the hotel, in the bar, on stage, off stage. But I just recently did Mozart's Sinfonia Concertante with Yuri Bashmet, and he is such a wonderful violist that it made me want to play string trios again."

In 1986, Mutter became the first holder of the International Chair of Violin Studies at the Royal Academy of Music in London. "For about three or four years, I spent quite a lot of time there, but now I am just head of the violin department and give master classes two or three times a year. They have some really gifted violinists. I concentrate on interpretation; it would make no sense to go into basic technical problems. You just have to deal with people's individual abilities and accomplishments. It's terribly difficult—and sometimes quite dangerous—to try to change the habits of 15 years or more. I don't think there is one ideal way of playing that is right for everybody."

Impressed by her unruffled composure under the pressure of a traveling schedule obviously crowded to the uttermost limits, I cannot resist a question I have often wanted to put to touring virtuosos. "How do you find time for everything you have to do—practice, rehearse, get a little rest, do a little sight-seeing, maybe wash your hair, buy a pair of stockings?"

"Well, I think I'm very well-organized." I can't help smiling at this understatement. "I really live by the clock: get up on time, have breakfast on time . . . that way, everything is possible. Before a concert, I always sleep in the afternoon, so I am well-rested no matter what I had to do in the morning, or the night before."

"When do you practice?"

"I am not a great practicer and actually haven't been since I started to concertize, because I learned to work with the score more than with the violin."

"But don't you have to keep up your technique, or practice the fast passages slowly sometimes to keep your fingers from running away?"

"Yes, but I am young; my fingers are in good shape. Once you have all the technical tools you need, you can solve your technical problems with the brain, the mind. Your imagination is more important than practicing a certain number of hours every day. Jimmy Levine [the music director of the Metropolitan Opera] said something very good the other day at Ravinia: 'Practice is supposed to make perfect, but really practice makes permanent.' You see? Besides, I am constantly playing, and whenever I know that something needs to be practiced, I do it, no matter what it is or where I might be. For example, when I had to learn the Rihm, I got up at six in the morning and went down into the basement to practice, because I didn't want to wake anybody up. It's no problem. If you really have to do something, you can always find a way."

"You mean you don't have to spend a lot of time maintaining your tools?"

She shakes her head decisively. "No, no—pure technique, that must be there; if it isn't, something is wrong."

How enviable, I think. "Well, I would think that only someone with a talent like yours can say that; I've known too many violinists who had reason to be afraid their tools would get rusty."

"Not yet—let's talk again in 20 or 30 years; maybe they do get rusty with age." We laugh, and she adds: "But of course, you can always get better, no question about it." I ask if she studied with anyone after Aida Stucki. "No, I never felt the need. I still go to her for advice and she often comes to my concerts. But I always learn from the great musicians I work with: the pianists, string players, and conductors. From my 13-year collaboration with Maestro von Karajan I gained so much insight into music generally that I can draw on it for a lifetime. And by now I can trust my own judgment about what I am doing."

Mutter has reduced the number of her yearly performances substantially in order to spend more time with her husband and her daughter, Arabella, who was born in 1991. At the close of our interview, I say that I'm looking forward to hearing her later that day and ask where she is going from New York. "Home!" she exclaims with her most radiant smile, "to my husband and my child."

Sarah Chang

*It's been barely a decade since the general public became aware of
Sarah Chang. She made her first public performances at age five,
and she hit a peak of popular adoration at the age of 12. Since
then, critics and music audiences around the world have praised
her growth from a virtuoso child into a young player who employs
her heart and mind as well as her fingers. At the start of a new century she is still not 20 years old, but her future as one of the emi-
nent soloists of her generation seems assured. She has graduated
from high school and from Juilliard Precollege, where she studied
with Dorothy DeLay. Having just won the 1999 Avery Fisher
Prize for musical excellence, she has put her college plans on hold
while she prepares for a busier-than-ever concert season.*

*No matter what one thinks of child prodigies and the some-
times relentless way in which they can be packaged for public con-
sumption, at 12 Chang had managed to retain a matter-of-fact and
engagingly childlike demeanor. The close mentoring she received
from both her parents and her famous teacher provided her with
a valuable measure of security and insulation during those early
years. This 1993 interview, held in the same year she won the
"Young Artist of the Year" award from Gramophone, provides a
glimpse of the way the young Chang approached the violin and
her public persona back when she was a pint-sized phenomenon.*

Child's Play

Stephanie von Buchau

Photo by Chris Lee

A mericans have always had a gushy, sentimental attitude toward
child prodigies, so the generalized cooing that greets Sarah Chang's
arrival on stage at San Francisco's Davies Symphony Hall is not unusu-
al. The orchestra's music director, Herbert Blomstedt, towers over the
12-year-old Chang. She is wearing a goldenrod ball gown that would
not be out of place in *Gone With the Wind*, with black patent-leather
Mary Jane shoes.

The audience reaction is not surprising, but Sarah Chang is. This is no stereotypical sprite. Take those Mary Janes, firmly planted some ways apart, as if she were claiming the stage for her own. Her feet don't move even during the most difficult parts of Paganini's Concerto No. 1 in D Major. Asked later about her rooted feet, Chang replies demurely, "Some violinists move around quite a bit, but Miss DeLay says I should get comfortable and then stay there."

Dorothy DeLay, the famed teacher who has nurtured several generations of superb violinists, including Itzhak Perlman, Shlomo Mintz, Cho-Liang Lin, Midori, and Nadja Salerno-Sonnenberg, has Chang under her wing as well. Though DeLay often travels with Chang, she

could not make this trip to San Francisco, but one doubts that she would have been surprised at her prodigy's performance. Even on a seven-eighths-size violin, Chang's sound is big and rich. Paganini's *cantilena*, obviously derived from Italian opera, induces a singing tone and legato that any soprano would envy. During the fiendish passagework, double-stops, and extravagant fioriture, the evenness of her tone is as remarkable as its flexibility. And when Chang produces the ghostly harmonics, the wit and spookiness of those disembodied high notes make many in the audience smile.

Near the end of the lengthy first movement, Chang introduces a monster cadenza by Emile Sauret, probably chosen by DeLay simply because her pupil can play the spots off of it. It doesn't add anything musically, but the Paganini concerto is more a matter of virtuoso technique and circus tricks anyway, so why not pile more whipped cream and a cherry on top of this high-calorie showpiece? During Chang's almost obscenely facile display of bravura fiddle playing, the orchestra's first violins and cellos, seated opposite each other, begin to lean forward, their mouths

Sarah Chang had full seasons of concert performances by the time she was 12.

agape. A few break out in goofy grins. These are tough, seasoned veterans of the concerto wars, and it is obvious that they have never heard anything like this before.

So is Sarah Chang surprising? You bet, because, while there have been amazing prodigies in our time—Menuhin and Midori, to name just two—I've certainly never encountered one with this kind of easy aplomb and casual self-assurance. At our interview in a tiny residential hotel near the San Francisco Performing Arts Center, there is nothing arrogant or self-aggrandizing about Chang. She is polite and answers questions readily, in grammatical, fully formed sentences. Except for an occasional giggle when some favorite nonmusical activity (such as shopping or horseback riding) is mentioned, she is a very grown-up young lady, aware of her value but not overwhelmed by it.

The *San Francisco Chronicle* music critic, while raving about Chang's San Francisco debut, did suggest that she was "now under full exploitation." Technically, this is true. No normal 12-year-old should be jetting around the world playing concerts with major symphony orchestras, no matter how talented she is. The avidity with which adults—her parents, teachers, record company, agents, managers, music directors, critics, and listeners—have attached themselves to this phenomenon can be unsettling to a thoughtful observer.

At the same time, the music business is business, and a 12-year-old genius is more marketable than an 18-year-old one. Keeping Chang out of the spotlight has no validity as long as she continues to play so superbly and suffers no physical or mental harm. Whether the relentless spotlight will encourage her further growth as a musician or accelerate premature burnout is anyone's guess. Yet at this moment, Chang may be surprising, but she is no freak show; she is a genuine, polished, artistic talent.

Barry Jekowsky, principal timpanist of the San Francisco Symphony and music director of the

Chang and Sir Colin Davis at a recording session of the Tchaikovsky Violin Concerto.

Enrico Ferorelli

California Symphony, conducted Chang's first-ever public performances of the Tchaikovsky and Sibelius violin concertos when she was just ten and 11 years old. He practically levitates when asked about her talent. "I don't know how you explain such a phenomenon, except that kids like this, who come along maybe once in 100 years, make the best case for reincarnation. I mean, where else could it come from? Not just the technique, but the musical soul that separates merely gifted children from extraordinary ones like Sarah?"

Her parents, Dr. Min Soo Chang, a violinist, and his wife, Myung Chang, a composer, immigrated to the United States from Korea in 1979. They settled in Philadelphia, where Sarah was born and began her violin studies at age four. She wanted to play her father's fiddle but says he wouldn't let her, "because kids have sticky fingers." Instead, Dr. Chang bought her a one-sixteenth size violin and taught her until she turned six, when he passed her on to DeLay at Juilliard. Since then she has traveled every Saturday to New York, where she studies a full musical curriculum in addition to her private lessons.

She also attends the Germantown Friends School in Philadelphia, where her favorite subjects are social studies and French. The Changs are adamant that she continue with regular school studies despite the extensive concertizing, and they try to incorporate education into her travels. Dr. Chang reports, "When I was a student I had to believe what it said in textbooks because I could not go there myself. But since Sarah

What she plays

Sarah Chang currently plays a full-size 1717 Giuseppe Guarneri del Gesù violin. At the time of this interview, however, she played a seven-eighths–size del Gesù (the "ex-Sennhauser") made in Cremona in the period 1733–1735. It has certificates from the Rudolph Wurlitzer Company (New York, 1930 and 1944), Adolph Möckel (Berlin, 1924), and Hamma and Company (Stuttgart, 1917). The instrument was loaned to her from the Stradivari Society of Chicago. Chang used strings by Dominant. She owns a gold-mounted Dominique Peccatte bow, but while playing the del Gesù, she used a modern bow by John Norwood Lee of Chicago.

does visit these places, we try to give her a book or guide so that she can study in advance. In the summer, we plan extra days after the concerts for sightseeing, museums, shopping. . . ."

His irrepressible daughter says, "I like shopping best!" but then adds seriously that she thinks that all this travel has helped her mature. "At school, my friends just read about Paris, London, Italy. But I actually get to go to those places. So, though the plane rides, the traveling, are very tiring, I am getting to do the things that my friends just dream about. And that makes me very lucky."

It is clear that Chang's parents and teacher are extraordinarily vigilant about protecting her from the unscrupulous and dangerous elements in today's world. Despite her maturity, a kind of innocence surrounds Chang like a shield; it makes an inquiring journalist think twice about how to phrase a question. She seems so wholesome, with her shiny black hair, bright eyes, and flawless complexion, that I can't help fantasizing that everyone who comes in contact with her must feel protective. Yet we know that celebrity in America has its ugly side: the stalkers, the flesh-pressers who claw for autographs. Is she affected by this?

Christian Steiner

"People are respectful," Chang answers. "Backstage, there are always those who look after me in case it gets a little too much, but mostly people are very nice. One of the things I like most about my career is the fan letters. I get interesting letters from all over the world. I just got one from Iraq. I'm touched that people take the time to write and tell me what they like. As for my school friends, they get excited about my trips. When I played for royalty in London when I was ten, they wanted to know what the duchess wore. They like hearing about where I've been and who I've met."

Chang's early talents have endured and matured with her.

Chang made her first public appearances as a violinist in the Philadelphia area when she was five, but she notes that her first appearance on television was as a gymnast at the same age. She says wistfully, "I can't do gymnastics anymore because my parents are afraid for my fingers. I didn't think about making the Olympics or anything like that, I just enjoyed it. I really like playing volleyball, but that's out, too."

At eight, Chang auditioned for Zubin Mehta, then music director of the New York Philharmonic. Mehta was so impressed that he asked her to appear as a surprise guest soloist at Avery Fisher Hall two days later. In 1991, the Philadelphia Orchestra's then-music director Riccardo Muti engaged her as a soloist for the orchestra's 90th-anniversary gala. Then Barry Jekowsky, who had conducted some of DeLay's pupils at

Recordings

Debut: Paganini, Tchaikovsky, Elgar, Sarasate, and others (EMI 7543522).

Mendelssohn: Concerto in E Minor; Sibelius: Concerto in D Minor. Berlin Philharmonic, Mariss Jansons, cond. (EMI 5564182).

Paganini: Concerto No. 1; Saint-Saëns: Havanaise, Introduction and Rondo Capriccioso. Philadelphia Orchestra, Wolfgang Sawallisch, cond. (EMI 5550262).

Simply Sarah: Encores by Brahms, Fauré, Mendelssohn, Prokofiev, Sarasate, and others (EMI 5561612).

Sweet Sorrow: Brahms, Lalo, Liszt, Paganini, Sibelius, Tchaikovsky, and others (EMI 5567912).

Tchaikovsky: Concerto; Brahms: Hungarian Dances. London Symphony Orchestra, Sir Colin Davis, cond. (EMI 7547532).

Vaughan Williams: The Lark Ascending. London Philharmonic, Bernard Haitink, cond. (EMI 5554872).

Vieuxtemps: Concerto No. 5; Lalo: Symphonie espagnole. Royal Concertgebouw and Philharmonia Orchestras; Charles Dutoit, cond. (EMI 5552922).

Aspen, suggested that Chang appear with his California Symphony in Walnut Creek. The sight of the tiny violinist whipping through Tchaikovsky and Sibelius so energized Jekowsky's audience that he has made it a point to include youthful soloists on his program ever since, as an educational tool. "Parents bring their kids and they see what is possible with hard work," he explains. "It gives everybody, musicians and audiences, a more positive view of the possibilities of classical music."

More guest appearances soon followed for Chang, at Ravinia with James Levine and the Chicago Symphony, at Saratoga with Charles Dutoit and the Philadelphia Orchestra, at Aspen with Pinchas Zukerman, and with the Pittsburgh and Montreal Symphonies. In October 1992, Chang made her European debut playing the Tchaikovsky Violin Concerto with the London Symphony Orchestra, with Sir Colin Davis conducting. They later recorded the concerto for EMI classics, which has an exclusive contract with Chang. Asked what it was like to work with such a distinguished array of music directors, Chang's answer is characteristically straightforward.

"Each conductor is different and has his own ideas and preferences about the music. So we talk to each other and work it out. For instance, take Charles Dutoit. I played the Paganini with him and our meetings were very casual, maybe just ten minutes the first time to get to know each other. With Sir Colin [Davis], our first meeting was much longer. I went to his house and we had something to eat, and then we really talked about the music. The meeting itself was longer, I believe, because of his personality. At the recording session we experimented quite a bit. We listened to takes in the control booth and discussed how to fix things, how to make them better. The kinds of things you discuss while recording are the same things we do for a concert. It isn't that different. Personally, I prefer the live concert, because it is more exciting."

Jekowsky claims that one of the delights of performing with Chang is her spontaneity. "It goes one way at the coaching sessions, another way at the rehearsal, and then it is totally different again at each performance. It is astonishing how she keeps coming up with fresh ways of looking at the music." Chang played five performances of the Paganini with the San Francisco Symphony in May and acknowledges that "different people have their opinions about which night went better, and I have my own" (which she coolly refuses to divulge).

Sometimes this matter-of-fact self-possession is a little spooky, so it is a relief when Chang giggles about school and about shopping, apparently her favorite nonmusical pastime. This makes her as all-American as any other mall rat. She reports that she and her friends enjoy light, comic movies rather than action or romance. She'd just seen *Home Alone II* and enjoyed it, but she adds with disdainful connoisseurship, "The first one was better." Another favorite activity is roller-blading; this confession draws a mild groan from her father, as everyone in the room imagines those priceless wrists being sprained. "My parents constantly worry about me falling and hurting my arm or hands. At home my mother makes me keep my room clean, but I don't have to do heavy chores!"

Chang seems to pack a lot of fun into a schedule that includes, in addition to school and concerts, a full Saturday at Juilliard, "where the special program, which starts at nine in the morning, includes classes in solfège, theory, ensemble, chamber music—everything for the complete musician. It isn't just violin lessons with Miss DeLay." (One of Chang's most charming conversational traits is her exquisite politeness of address. It is always "Miss DeLay," "Mr. Jekowsky," or "Sir Colin." In that, of course, she is not the typical American kid.)

One might assume that DeLay gives special consideration to Sarah because Dr. Chang is her teaching assistant. But Chang assesses her teacher's care with shrewd insight. "Miss DeLay is simply amazing. She just had her 76th birthday, and she has so much energy. Every day she goes to Juilliard and every other week to Cincinnati, and she travels with me whenever she can. She is concentrating on me as a performer now, but she has hundreds of students and she cares about each one of them the same way she does about me. She is wonderful to all of us."

Still, the relationship is special, and you glimpse it when Chang talks about her violins. "My parents worried about the tone when I recorded *Debut* for EMI, because apparently nobody had ever made a recording before on a quarter-size violin. But it turned out well, I think. My half-size violin, the one on which I made a lot of debuts, was from Charles Beare in London. He said that he absolutely had to have it back, as he had become very attached to it. The problem was that I fell in love with it too, and I really wanted that instrument, just for possession, even after I was playing a larger size. But it didn't work out and I had to give it back."

The love story of her young life so far? She laughs, "Yes, I think it was; I wanted that violin so badly. But there's my three-quarter–size that I got from Miss DeLay. It had been in her attic for 45 years. It hadn't been played, and it wasn't in very good condition. The weather changes alone in that period of time are very hard on a violin. But we had it fixed, and I was very happy with it. I became so attached to it that Miss DeLay said I could keep it; it is still in my closet at home. When I was searching for a three-quarter, before Miss DeLay gave me hers, people everywhere from America to London kept offering to let me try this one or that one. But I hate it when you have to give them back! It is really hard to part with a violin after you have come to know it. The seven-eighths size that I play now is on loan from [the Stradivari Society in] Chicago. I've been playing it for a year and now I am beginning to experiment until I find the full-sized instrument that I will always use. In about a year, I think I'll be ready." (See page 32.)

Her father suggests that she get the del Gesù from her room, and she

produces a battered canvas case holding the precious violin, several
bows, and three lucky photos (shots of Chang with her grandmother
and younger brother, Michael). Asked how she chooses a bow, she says
seriously, "The bow is even more personal than a violin. Everybody
must choose his or her own style. Miss DeLay says that the bow is strict-
ly up to the player because everyone's hand is different. The bow is so
personal because, after all, it is your sound. Different people want different things from a bow. The balance, the weight, the sound. . . . Also,
you use different bows for different sizes of violins and also because of
the music. You can use a lighter bow for Mozart than you would for
Tchaikovsky. Older bows are prettier, but I am
using this modern [John Lee bow] now."

Asked how she maintains her nails, she
shrugs. "Nothing special except to file the left
hand, because I don't want to snap a string. I've
never actually broken a string in performance,
but I know it will happen some day. You can't
have a whole career without a broken string, but
I don't worry about it. If it happens, there is nothing you can do. It's funny, because if you try to
break a string, you can't do it. It just won't snap.
But if it wants to snap, usually because of the
weather, there is nothing you can do to stop it."

Chang playing with the
New York Philharmonic
under Kurt Masur in
1995.

Chang has played a lot of outdoor concerts and knows their special
problems. "Tuning, of course," she says. "In Aspen there is almost no
humidity, but in Philadelphia or Washington, D.C., it is so hot and
sticky. I played in Washington outdoors two years ago [1991]. I was
absolutely boiling, my strings were sliding, and my fingers were wet.
Outdoor concerts pose more of a risk, but it is also more exciting and
more casual and I like that. I also like playing for a lot of people. Once
my mom was in the middle of an outdoor audience and she said she
could hardly see me, I was so far away. I looked like a peanut!"

So, when Sarah Chang grows up, does she want to be a violinist? Dr.
Chang gives a hearty laugh, but Sarah, with her customary aplomb,
replies, "Yes, I think so. Right now I want to go on with it, but look at
[Fritz] Kreisler. He was a composer, a violinist, a soldier, and a doctor,
and he was well-known for all those activities. Right now, I think I will
be a violinist when I grow up, but you never know."

Just don't bet the farm against it.

Kennedy

The English violinist Kennedy—formerly known as Nigel Kennedy—has been among the world's leading virtuosos for some two decades. He began his career firmly grounded in the classical repertoire, studying at the Sir Yehudi Menuhin School in England and then with Dorothy DeLay at the Juilliard School in New York City.

In this 1989 interview, however, Kennedy made it clear that he didn't want to be tied to any single genre. He has been quoted as saying, "People can say I'm a classical violinist if they want to, but I've always viewed myself as a musician who plays music, and not just a certain part of it." In 1992 he took a sabbatical from classical music (saying he didn't want to play anything by "dead composers"), and when he returned to the concert stage in April 1997, he reemphasized his coexisting interest in jazz and rock. Nevertheless, his return was huge news in the classical-music world. Critics who had scorned him for his departure now greeted him as though he were the prodigal son, and his performances of the staple repertoire were greeted with high praise.

Now living in London, Kennedy performs and records widely, alone and with his ensemble, the Kennedy Collective, which plays music ranging from Bach to Bartók to Hendrix.

Ready for Anything

Timothy Pfaff

What Nigel Kennedy likes most about his 1707 Stradivari violin is that "you can play anything on it." Kennedy does not mean anything from Bach to Berio; he means anything he's inclined to play, which at this point includes equal amounts of jazz and rock music. At 30, British-born Kennedy already is his homeland's preeminent classical fiddler; he also is rapidly consolidating a reputation as one of the most gifted concert violinists of any nationality on the international scene. But what classical music lovers are only beginning to realize is that Kennedy is making a bid for recognition as "the compleat musician."

Increasing numbers of the world's top classical musicians are turning out so-called "crossover" recordings, as much for the lucrative prof-
its involved as for new avenues of artistic expression, or at least so it
would appear. Kennedy's is not a "crossover" story. In fact, one of his
first formal attempts to bridge the gap between classical and popular
music was starting a group called Crossover. He was so dissatisfied at
the level of musical interaction obtainable from musicians of different
stripes that he disbanded the group before its first scheduled performance. And while the idea hasn't been entirely abandoned, for the
moment Kennedy seems content to participate in various kinds of
music making, each in its own venue.

"I've always enjoyed audiences," he commented a decade ago in an
interview. "I think playing jazz and rock has raised my consciousness
about my duty to my audience. In classical music, and particularly in
recording situations, there's the danger of leaving the audience aspect
out. I feel a definite duty towards my audience: to communicate."

On this morning in January 1989, after his rapturously received duo
recital with pianist Ken Noda at Hertz Hall on the campus of the
University of California, Berkeley, a tired-but-exhilarated Kennedy
seems eager to talk about all the facets of his musical life. His enthusiasm about his instruments—he also plays a Bellosio viola and Barcus-
Berry electric violin (to compete with other amplified instruments in
rock groups)—is a natural way in. The way he talks about the Stradivari
is, to say the least, revelatory.

"It's really a beautiful fiddle, in mint condition. It's had a new neck
put on it for the higher pitch of the modern concert halls, but that's it.
[While not quite a gift, Kennedy's Stradivari came to him from a woman
music lover in what he calls 'a mutually beneficial business arrangement.'] Before I got it, it was called the 'Cathedral.' Now it's called the
'Animal.' I've rechristened it to live today. I don't want everything I play
to have to be 'religious' music—and 'Animal' sounds more like the biz,
don't you think?"

"Animal" and "monster" may well be displacing "cool" and "like" as
the most frequently used words in the spike-haired, punk-clad musician's Brighton-accented vocabulary. All performances, in any venue,
are "gigs." What becomes clear, however, is that Kennedy's persona is an
artful combination of ruse and utter seriousness about what he's doing.

His working-class manner, for example, may be part affectation—or
compensation for the boyish, hypersensitive, "pale Brit" look that
graced his early classical album covers. But the matter-of-fact approach
also reflects his having descended from a family of performing musicians. His mother was a piano teacher; his grandfather was a cellist who
played chamber music with Heifetz, Kreisler, and Primrose; and his
father was also a cellist, with the Royal Philharmonic (in which he also
performed concertos under the baton of Sir Thomas Beecham).

Young Kennedy's own attitude about the profession of music making could hardly be more down-to-earth. "Everyone's got music in them," he says, "and anyone who enjoys music has the possibility of playing. It just depends on whether they're willing to put up with the discipline it takes. You have to work. That's life, isn't it? I just prefer to work doing what I'm doing over any other job."

The morning of our interview, Kennedy disembarks the elevator of Berkeley's Shattuck Hotel in basic black and white—a long black coat, workman's boots, and what might best be described as dress thermal underwear. His punk look gives evidence of being as much an artistic as a fashion statement. Kennedy first realized that music was a means of communication—and potentially his voca-tion—"when I was 13 or 14 and met Stéphane Grappelli. It was about that age, the normal rebel years of a teenager, when I discovered that music was something central to my life. At the time I was having a bit of trouble with my teachers, because I was finding that I could go out on stage and ignore everything I'd been taught and just play to the audience—and they'd like it. I think in music you've got to be a bit of a rebel all your life, because you have to set your own values. Otherwise there's no point in doing it. So it's an excuse for being a teenager for life."

Steve Rapport

In the late 1980s, Nigel Kennedy began to rebel against his image as the darling of the classical-music world.

Kennedy won a scholarship to the Yehudi Menuhin School, in piano, at the age of seven. There his interests changed to violin and, to the dismay of some of his teachers, to jazz. Menuhin's own fabled catholicity of musical taste ("He's always had an open attitude to most kinds of music, although he's got a block with rock—doesn't like the drums," Kennedy says) prompted an introduction to Grappelli, whose protégé Kennedy soon became. Kennedy made his Carnegie Hall debut with Grappelli at the age of 17.

"I started in classical because my mum was a piano teacher. I started playing just for fun, and she gave me lessons before I went to school. And at the Menuhin School, at least until I was 12 or 13, it was a classical situation too. A lot of jazz and rock musicians don't start play-ing until they're 12 or 13 anyway, so I have to say that my background is similar to theirs.

"I find that a lot of people in my audience who aren't musicians start-ed by listening to rock bands as teenagers. Then, when they got sick of the shortage of decent album material, they got into jazz. And when they got even more into the structural things, they got into classical. I've kind of done it the other way around. Half Australian, that's why. My dad and grandad were from there. Bad news, all them dingos. I'm glad I was born in Britain," he adds with a robust laugh.

About the time of his Carnegie debut with Grappelli, Kennedy entered New York's Juilliard School, where he studied for two and a half

What he plays

At the time of this interview, Kennedy's various instruments included a 1707 Antonio Stradivari (generally known as the "Cathedral," although he has dubbed it the "Animal"), an Anselmo Bellosio viola, and a Barcus-Berry electric violin.

More recently he has been playing a 1735 del Gesù with a Finkel bow. He uses Dominant strings with a Westminster E. He has an English viola "of no great provenance—the proper size, however" (his previous viola was fairly small). He also has an electric violin made by David Bruce Johnson of Birmingham, England.

Andrew Catlin

years. "I was there too long," he says, "but not long enough to get a diploma. I was already getting gigs, and nobody was asking me for my diploma, so I decided it was time to stop. I didn't like the school, where the concentration was mainly on technical things. I could have become disillusioned by the scene, but playing jazz down in the clubs kept me in music." He did prolong his study with Dorothy DeLay—"a gold mine of information, that lady." But, he adds, "I don't really work with anyone now. I find that I get a lot of feedback from my colleagues, and that's the way I like to do it. I always preferred the learning experience of doing something, making mistakes, and learning from them. That's what you can do with live playing."

New York, the international center of violin playing, remains the Kennedy base for now [since this interview, he has moved back to London]. "I feel American," he allows. "I've come here because I feel like the values of this country are in common with mine. I belong here, in a way, particularly in my situation as a musician. There are more young people here trying to do things similar to what I'm doing."

Kennedy now divides his concertizing more or less evenly between the U.S. and the U.K. He plays fewer than the 120 concerts per year that first characterized his schedule, but classical gigs still take him everywhere. What other music he makes has depended on which side of the Atlantic he's on.

"London's very good for rock music," he explains. "Lots of musicians hanging out there, so I tend to play more rock. Here, more jazz. It's not like there's no good jazz players in Europe, but the general standard here is so much higher. Jazz is much more in people's blood from an earlier age. The same with R&B and blues. There are good groups in every city I go to. It's very exciting. I'm getting a jazz group together here and am going to start touring with it."

The versatile violinist has often commented that it is in many ways more difficult to make the transition from Walton to Vivaldi, for example, than from Ravel to jazz or rock. Without particularly intending to, Kennedy proved his point in 1984 with what turned out to be a pair of recordings for the Chandos label. Having completed a stunning recording of the Elgar Violin Sonata and seven other, shorter Elgar pieces a few hours early, he and pianist Peter Pettinger, also a superb jazz player, repaired to a local pub. After a drink, they discovered that they still wanted to play and convinced their producer, Brian Couzens, to return to the studio with them. Entirely spontaneously, and completely unrehearsed, they laid down seven tracks of jazz standards released on a remarkable disc called *Nigel Kennedy Plays Jazz*. Listening to them back to back, it's difficult to believe that Kennedy is playing the same instrument on both, so distinctive and idiomatic for jazz is the sound he draws from it.

He now has an exclusive and unprecedented contract with both the classical and pop divisions of EMI/Angel. For the moment, though, the only EMI recording in which American audiences can test the fluidity with which Kennedy moves between idioms is the pairing of "Mainly Black," his own arrangement of music from Duke Ellington's ambitious *Black, Brown, and Beige* suite, and the Bartók Solo Violin Sonata. To Kennedy, the pairing seemed logical for reasons beyond the fact that the two works both received their premieres in Carnegie Hall (in 1943 and 1944, respectively, with Menuhin in the Bartók). More important to him, both represent their composers' unique capacities for translating music from their own respective backgrounds into larger, structurally tighter forms. Calling Ray Nance's contribution to Ellington's 1958

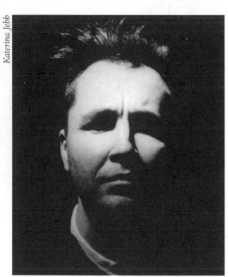

Katerina Jebb

recording of *Black, Brown, and Beige* "some of the most beautiful violin playing I have ever heard," Kennedy transcribed it into his own arrangement, in which he elaborated on the original.

EMI recordings thus far available in England include only a rock album, *Nigel Kennedy: Let Loose,* featuring original compositions and arrangements made in collaboration with Dave Heath; *Experiment IV,* with Kate Bush ("one of my most rewarding experiences in music so far," he stated in 1987); and violin solos on Paul McCartney's *Once Upon a Long Ago* and new *Talk Talk* album. It wasn't wasted on Kennedy that McCartney liked "my simplest things best." Recently, American concert audiences have had the opportunity to hear his arrangements of Beatles songs. Reverence comes into his voice as he contemplated what the Fab Four were able to do with three-minute songs, and, he comments

In the late 1990s the violinist dropped his given name and performed as Kennedy.

matter-of-factly, "I think *Sgt. Pepper's Lonely Hearts Club Band* is some of the most influential music of the century."

"The feel is the main thing," he says in summary. "The more kinds of music you play, the more open you are to the diversity of things you want to express. Any music you play should be happening now as if for the first time only. In jazz, that's the feeling you have to have, otherwise you're not doing the business. In classical, you should have it too, but you can get away without doing the business.

"In the nonclassical kinds of music I play, people go for expressive values, which by definition change according to the kind of expression you need. In classical music, it sometimes seems that technical values are imposed on young musicians before they know what they want to do with expression. It's not altogether a good thing to learn technique first. If you choose to play a piece, it should be because you love it and think you can communicate it. Then you can master it technically.

"Charlie Parker first picked up the sax after hearing Lester Young play. He got his ideas first, and then the technique came. The same was true with people like Heifetz and Rubinstein—Rachmaninoff, too. It happens that way around with the great musicians. But the bulk of the factory-produced musicians in New York learn technique first. They're short of ideas because they've got such a rigid sense of what the instrument should do."

If anything, it's the superabundance of Kennedy's musical ideas that fuels his work now. When not on the road, he practices at least four hours a day. "Time has to be spent doing it, so I do it," he notes dispassionately. "You don't have to use a lot of grey cells to do most of that work, so usually I put a quiz show or a hockey game on the telly and just hack my violin. Finger exercises mostly, physical coordination stuff. Everyone has their own weaknesses and strengths, so I've made up my own exercises to deal with my problems.

"If you can do the simple things well, then you have the basis for being more ambitious. It's mainly the bowing, getting control of the pressure and speed of the bow, making sure that it's going in the right direction and parallel with the bridge and all that. If you practice regularly, you get a natural feel for it. The other fundamental is playing in tune—something you'll be developing for the rest of your life. Of course it's easier to play in tune on the piano, but on the fiddle you have the possibility of playing more in tune. You can play an F-sharp as an F-sharp, instead of mistaking it as G-flat, which is going in another direction. But that's a life's work."

Kennedy has yet to record Bach [see his updated discography on page 48], but, he insists, "I need to play a bit of Bach at least three or four times a week. Bach really awakens your instincts, heightens your sensitivity to harmony and melody. I think he's the ultimate Romantic composer, really. All his structural and harmonic things are the roots of what's good in Romantic music."

Kennedy seems determined to achieve as great a spontaneity in the studio as in the concert hall. "In the old days," he notes, "people like Rubinstein and Kreisler and Casals recorded the pieces they had a real relationship with. That's the way I think it still should be. When I go into the studio, I want to represent everything I can of what I think of the piece at that time. I want it to be an all-time experience, not my first thoughts on a piece. After that, I no longer feel tied down. When I leave the recording studio, I feel a new burst of creative activity. When you feel you've done your best with a piece, then you no longer have to do quite the same thing with it any more."

It was his landmark recording of the Elgar Violin Concerto with Vernon Handley and the London Philharmonic Orchestra, the first concerto record to win *Gramophone*'s Record of the Year award in 1984, that catapulted Kennedy into international celebrity. He doesn't worry about overplaying it "because the conductor is so responsible for the structure that you never get it the same way twice. It's got to be a great partnership to make that piece work. Whereas the fiddle player is more

Recordings

Bach: *Sonatas and Partitas, BWV 1001–1006;* Beethoven: *Concerto, Op. 61.* North German RSO, Klaus Tennstedt, cond. (EMI Classics CDC 54574).

Bartók: *Sonata* (EMI CDC 47621).

Brahms: *Concerto.* London Philharmonic Orchestra, Klaus Tennstedt, cond. (EMI CDC 54187).

Bruch: *Concerto No. 1;* Mendelssohn: *Concerto, Op. 64;* Schubert: *Rondo, D. 438.* English Chamber Orchestra, Jeffrey Tate, cond. (EMI CDC 49663).

Classic Kennedy *(forthcoming in February 2000, on EMI Classics).*

Elgar: *Chanson de matin, Chanson de nuit.* With Peter Pettinger, piano (Chandos 8380).

Elgar: *Concerto.* London Philharmonic, Vernon Handley, cond. (EMI CDM 63795).

Ellington/arr. Kennedy: *Mainly Black.* With Alec Dankworth, double bass (EMI CDC 47621).

The Kennedy Experience: *Music by Jimi Hendrix, arr. Kennedy* (Sony 61687).

Kennedy Plays Kreisler: *Lotus Land, Liebesleid, and others* (EMI CDC 56626).

Nigel Kennedy Plays Jazz: *Music of Jackson, Mercer, Wonder, Reinhardt/Grappelli, and others.* With Peter Pettinger, piano (Chandos 6513).

Salut d'Amour: *Music of Elgar, including Sonata; Sospiri; Mot d'amour, Op. 13; Canto popolare; Six Very Easy Pieces in the First Position, Op. 22.* With Peter Pettinger, piano (Chandos 8380).

Sibelius: *Concerto;* Tchaikovsky: *Concerto.* City of Birmingham Symphony Orchestra, Simon Rattle, cond.; London Philharmonic Orchestra, O. Kamu, cond. (EMI CDC 54559).

Vivaldi: *Concertos, Op. 8/1–4; The Four Seasons.* English Chamber Orchestra, Nigel Kennedy, soloist and cond. (EMI CDC 56253).

Walton: *Concerto for Violin, Concerto for Viola.* Royal Philharmonic Orchestra, André Previn, cond. (EMI CDC 49628).

responsible for the structure in the Mendelssohn, the pacing of things and the relationship between the soloist and the orchestra." Having played the Mendelssohn countless times, and now having recorded it, Kennedy accepts engagements to play it only when he senses the potential for a real partnership with orchestra and conductor.

"I look for that always," he continues. "It's a more difficult balance than with a pianist, because the conductor's got a hard job on his hands controlling all those heathens playing in the orchestra. But with the right conductor and orchestra, it can be really exhilarating, because suddenly you've got communication with 70 or 80 people and the conductor, and that's really a high. If you're going to be playing the same concerto for the rest of your life, you're definitely going to be looking for something different from a conductor to make it work, to make it more than a repeat performance. You've got to be a positive animal."

Asked about his attitude toward cadenzas, the same word surfaces. "Animal. I write my own for concertos that don't have one written, and even if they do, I usually end up putting a bit of my own

In the late 1990s, Kennedy's multigenre talents are established.

stuff in them. I like improvising, but one of my cadenzas in the Brahms got pretty out of hand one time. And the first time I ever tried to improvise a cadenza in Mozart, I ended up in the wrong key, with it sounding like Debussy. Bad news to have a shortage of musical ideas and get into a circle of fifths and forget where you started. That's when I decided to have some structure for the cadenza before I go out on the stage. I usually write out a thematic structure and then let things go in between. I think that's a truthful way of doing it. I think it's valid for a performer to bring his own knowledge into a cadenza and make it sound like now. That's what we should be doing."

For the most part, however, jazz and rock seem satisfactory outlets for his urge to compose. He's tentatively begun investigating the commissioning of new music for the classical side but was chary of naming composers.

"I'm not more concerned about one field than the others," he says. "Sometimes I get real cool jazz musicians wondering why I'm doing the classical stuff. Winton Marsalis wonders why I play rock. So you have these prejudices in every field. But they're much less than what they were before. If it were ten or 20 years ago, someone probably couldn't have become as totally involved in music as I am without some retribution. So we're getting closer to having our cake and eating it, aren't we?" With a deep laugh, he concludes, "That will do nicely."

Midori

Midori is now in her second decade of an international career that took off with a burst of publicity when she was still a child. She has shown that not all prodigies burn out early, and that a technically advanced child can turn into a musically insightful and expressive adult performer.

In this 1995 interview, Midori was looking forward enthusiastically to a summer spent playing chamber music at the Marlboro Music Festival in Vermont. Her eagerness proved prophetic; since that summer she has increasingly made room for chamber music in her performance schedule, playing with such musicians as violist Nobuko Imai, cellist Peter Wiley, and, of course, her longtime pianist and musical collaborator Robert McDonald.

In addition to her performances, her work with the foundation Midori and Friends, founded in 1992, has increased since she affectionately described the organization in the interview below. Concentrating on select New York City public elementary schools, the foundation's programs include teacher training, family concerts, and an instrument-lending program. Midori continues to involve other artists, from renowned soloists such as Emanuel Ax and Yefim Bronfman to young ensembles, and she participates in many of the programs herself.

Coming of Age

by Edith Eisler

Midori—the name has become a household word, but who can remember her surname? Like Solomon, the great English pianist, she decided that she wanted to be known by her first name alone. It proved to be a brilliant idea, because it differentiated her so thoroughly from all other violinists. Born in Osaka, Japan, she moved to New York in 1982 to study with Dorothy DeLay at the Juilliard School of Music. The same year, her debut in the Paganini Concerto at the New York Philharmonic's New Year's Gala, under Zubin Mehta, created a sensation and started a new wave of musical prodigies. She was 11 years old.

Her most widely reported appearance took place in Tanglewood four years later, at a concert with the Boston Symphony under Leonard Bernstein. In the middle of the performance, she broke a string and, as is customary in such cases, exchanged instruments with the concertmaster. But that wasn't all: a string broke on the replacement violin as well, necessitating another switch. Although her own violin was smaller, she adjusted her intonation to both new instruments instantly. With unperturbed, confident poise and without missing a note, she finished the piece, and the audience, having watched in spellbound disbelief, erupted into applause.

Sheila Rock

Now in her twenties, Midori has thoroughly shed her child-prodigy image.

I first heard Midori in what she calls her "official" Philharmonic debut in the Dvořák Concerto a few years later. Captivated by her radiant talent, I have attended her concerts ever since and watched her grow from a young prodigy into a still young but constantly developing and maturing performer. Shortly before this interview, she gave a most impressive performance of works by Bach, Beethoven, Schubert, and Szymanowski on the concert series in the late Anne Ratner's home in New York. Our conversation (conducted in my home, where she had been gracious enough to meet with me) ranged far and wide, from her early training to her present interests. But we focused particularly on a subject very much on my mind: growing up as a prodigy, and growing out of being a prodigy. Though this can be a sensitive topic, she was willing to discuss it with great frankness and candor.

When did you begin playing?

I received my first violin—a very small one—as a gift on my third birthday. I had asked for it; I already knew I wanted to play. My mother [teacher and performer Setsu Goto] is a violinist, and she started me when I was four—that seems old these days, doesn't it? I can't say how many years I studied with her. We never had a formal teacher-student relationship; I feel I never really stopped studying with her. Even after I was officially working with Dorothy DeLay at Juilliard, my mother helped me with my practicing. Now she just comes to some of my concerts in New York. We no longer live together, although we still live in the same building, and she looks after my two dogs for me whenever I'm on tour.

How and when did you first come to America?

In the summer of 1981, my mother and I were invited to the Aspen Music Festival. When I was about seven or eight, a friend of my mother's, who was also a violinist, came back to Japan from New York to give a concert. She heard me practice, got interested, and told my mother she wanted to take a tape of my playing back to America. A neighbor of hers was an assistant of Dorothy DeLay's; she played it to him and he took it to Miss DeLay, who put Aspen in touch with us. I was about nine years old, and my mother was beginning to think I should study formally with a teacher, so meeting Miss DeLay that summer came at just the right time. I went to her at Juilliard the following year. I studied with her for about five years; that was the only formal training I had.

What sort of pieces did you play when you came to Miss DeLay?

I had studied some major concertos by that time. After I started working with her, I learned some brand-new ones, but mostly I relearned those I knew already.

Susan Johann

You must have practiced an awful lot when you were very young. I've talked to a number of former prodigies about how they grew up, but always many years later. You are the first one who's young enough to remember what it's like.

Well, I'm 23, but go ahead, ask me questions.

Midori with her pianist and friend Robert McDonald.

How many hours did you practice at the beginning?

That I don't remember; in fact, I don't remember much about what I did when I was so young.

Did you like practicing?

[*Pauses.*] Well, if I had really disliked it, I don't think I would have done it. I may not have loved it, but I don't think I needed to be pushed. So I wouldn't say I didn't like to practice. Also, my mother has a special way of teaching young children. She very much encourages them to learn pieces they want to play, within their abilities; she doesn't force them to play pieces they don't like unless it's absolutely necessary for developing their technique.

Once you were at Juilliard, did you go to school, too?

Yes, I went to the Professional Children's School, because it has a flexible schedule. At that time, they had a lot of actors and actresses and models, and not as many musicians as they do now; they also didn't have as many non–English-speaking kids. Now they have a very strong English as a Second Language department, but I never even took English as a second language.

You sound as if English were your first language.

Thank you! [*Smiles.*] I completed my regular education at Professional Children's School and graduated from its high school. At Juilliard, I went to the Pre-College Division; I never made it into the upper school, because you have to be of college age and I left when I was 15. I had classes all day Saturday—theory, solfège, orchestra, piano—and I had one, sometimes two, lessons during the week.

Did you also study with any of Miss DeLay's assistants?

Amelia V. Panico

Only toward the end, for maybe seven months, with Jens Ellermann. He no longer teaches at Juilliard, but he has a splendid class in Hanover, Germany. But even during that time, Miss DeLay saw me once a week. Some students got scheduled lessons with her every two weeks and an assistant every week. In my case, it was the opposite: I saw Mr. Ellermann every other week—just to do the basics, like scales and exercises—and her every week. She was my main teacher. I prepared a different concerto for every lesson, memorized and rehearsed with a pianist; I always tried to achieve performance level. Of course, if I had allowed myself more time, I would have given better performances, but I only very rarely repeated a concerto for two consecutive lessons.

Didn't you run out of concertos very soon at that rate?

Well, then I'd do them again. I went through all the major ones and back again.

Midori made her name as a soloist but has become increasingly interested in chamber music.

Weren't you also playing concerts at the same time?

Yes, but I wasn't just bringing the concertos I performed to the lessons. You see, when you start appearing in public, you play much the same pieces in different places for several months. The first year, I had about 20 or 30 concerts, but I played only the Mendelssohn and Paganini Concertos. So besides practicing those, I was preparing other concertos for the lessons as well.

How many hours a day did you practice during that time?

At least five.

Here is what, to me, is the most crucial question: Learning all these difficult, complicated pieces so quickly when you were so young, did you think you had a chance to develop your own ideas, your own feelings about the music?

There was no time. I mean, it's not that anyone stopped me from doing it, but there just isn't enough time to think and feel through a piece of music when you prepare a new concerto every week. In addition, I was going to school full time and doing at least three or four hours of homework every night. People often mistakenly assume that going to a school like Professional Childrens' School means you can practice your craft instead of going to classes and doing your homework. But it was good for me to go through this kind of training, because it made me very relaxed in my later years, when I had to perform and study different concertos at the same time. It taught me to learn pretty fast.

I feel I really started to learn about music when I was about 14 or 15, going to operas and concerts, listening to recordings, applying what I knew to my music. I wasn't just playing the violin and then having a life; it sort of became connected. To a certain extent it probably always was, because I used music as a form of expression, but now it all started to come together: the knowledge of history and culture and theory, the experience of playing in concerts, as well as personal experiences. And when I left Juilliard, it opened up so much free time, and it made me really think for myself; that's what was so good about it. I had to be my own teacher, to develop my ears, to be very critical. It was a very positive experience.

Very few people would have the courage and sense of adventure to want to be independent at the age of 15.

I've never been afraid of adventure.

Did you feel that leaving school made it possible to catch up with your fingers?

Yes, I did feel that. It was one of the reasons I wanted to leave. I studied at Juilliard—that was very good; I studied with DeLay—that was excellent. I learned a lot, but it was time for me to leave.

So after you left, you continued to study on your own.

Of course. I was already performing, but I had guidance from various people: Isaac Stern gave me private lessons, not on a regular basis, but he has influenced me a lot over the years, and [pianist] Bob [McDonald] has been another strong influence since we started playing together seven years ago. I also tried to study the other works of the composers whose pieces I was playing, to immerse myself in their style, their musical language and its character; that makes a difference in my interpretations. I feel my playing has been changing quite a bit. My priorities are so much more musical now than they used to be, but I think that is possible because I don't have to worry as much about technique. I feel that communication is the key to a successful performance, not the display of technical abilities.

Then there's the experience of performing. You know that's worth

Uhat she plays

Midori plays two violins, a 1735 Giusieppe Guarneri del Gesù called the "David" (not to be confused with the "David" Heifetz played), which she owns, and a 1722 Antonio Stradivari called the "Jupiter," which is on permanent loan to her [as of this book's publication, she is playing exclusively on the del Gesù].

"The Guarneri was loaned to me through a private collector in Chicago, and a couple of years later, she was generous enough to sell it to me at a very reasonable price," says Midori. "And the Strad—that was really wonderful—is on loan to me for life from a very good family friend who just said, 'Choose a violin and we'll buy it.' It came from a dealer in Germany through another dealer in New York.

"The Strad is bigger than normal, while the Guarneri is smaller," she adds. How does she play in tune? "I never change violins from day to day. At the moment, I play more on the 'David,' partly because it's easier. I used it last week, for example, when I recorded the Tchaikovsky Concerto. But the 'Jupiter' is a gorgeous instrument, in wonderful condition, one of the finest available examples of Stradivari's work. I played on it for the recording of the Sibelius Concerto."

Midori owns a number of bows: a Pierre Simon, an A. Lamy, and an F.N. Voirin (listed in her own order of preference). "I also have a Peccatte," she adds, "but it's last on the list because it's too light. I got it when I was rather young and outgrew it."

She uses Goldbrokat or Pirastro Synoxa strings on the E string, and Dominant medium-gauge strings on the others.

Brigitte Lacombe

thousands of hours of practicing. I could perform the same concertos 100 times a year, and I would still play them differently every time; I have a different feeling every day of my life. And as I get to know the pieces better, I've become more spontaneous, I'm taking more chances, leaving more to chance on stage—not technically speaking, but musically. Knowing myself better as a human being has also had an important impact on my music making.

Yes, it has definitely been my impression over the years that you have become more free emotionally. And obviously you love performing.
Oh, yes!

Is it difficult to start performing as a prodigy because of the expectations it raises, both in yourself and in the audience?
Yes, but it also gives you the invaluable experience of having a standard and the opportunity to share ideas, not only with an audience, but on a professional level with conductors and other musicians. I think it's wonderful.

Do you get nervous?
No.

You never did?
Never!

Not even tense?
Tense—in what sense?

I don't mean technically—inwardly.
[*Pauses.*] Not really, but even if I do feel a little tense, I have the calmness in me to control it. But there have been concerts when I felt that the people around me got very nervous. I remember before my first Carnegie Hall recital, which was being videotaped by Sony Classical, a couple of people from management came in looking haggard, with circles under their eyes [*laughs*], and before I played with Mehta for the first time, the people around me were looking totally blue. But I myself don't get nervous.

Did your career develop quickly or gradually?
Very quickly; you know, I've only been playing professionally for about 12 years. I've been with the same management, ICM Artists, since the beginning. I guess I've been very fortunate. For example, I didn't tell myself that I had to break that string at Tanglewood. . . .

No? It would have been such a good stunt!
[*Laughs.*] I didn't ask for it, but that's what people keep talking about.

Well, if that were the only thing, or even the most remarkable thing, you've done, it wouldn't have gotten you very far. And you started off by playing concertos with orchestras?

Yes. I began to play recitals when I was about 13 or 14. I learned most of the sonata literature after I was 15, but at first, my recital programs were mixed: for example, a Mozart and a Prokofiev sonata, and Sarasate's *Carmen Fantasie* to end with. Right now, I do heavy programs like the one you heard at Anne's; that was the first time we performed it, and the first time I learned the Schubert Fantasy.

Do you find it difficult?

Very difficult, yes.

Even you—I'm so glad to hear that!

But it's so beautiful, I just love it. Our next program at Avery Fisher Hall is quite interesting, heavily Eastern European, with Schnittke and Bartók, and a Szymanowski piece I love; it's the last of a set of three short works jointly known as *Mythes,* and it is gorgeous. You know, Bob [McDonald] and I go to Poland frequently; we were there again last January, and I really love the country. I went to a music store about the size of this room and bought two boxes full of music, among other things the complete works of Szymanowski and Lutoslawski. I've become very interested in Szymanowski; there is a beautiful opera, *King Roger,* and two violin concertos and a sonata that I'd love to play.

Do you have any other favorite composers?

Well, I love Elgar—I play both his Concerto and Sonata—Tchaikovsky, Dvořák. . . . I try to keep learning new pieces. I just started on the first Shostakovich concerto a few days ago; it's wonderful and I'm very excited. I'm going to record it soon. I just came back from recording the Tchaikovsky with the Berlin Philharmonic under Claudio Abbado. It was done live, which I much prefer to recording in the studio.

You tour a lot, don't you?

Yes, but I've cut down my performing schedule. For several years, until about two years ago, I played maybe 95 or 100 concerts a year; now it's only about 80. I want to have time for many other things, because an important part of my life is outside the profession. In January, I started on an independent study course at New York University, which means I don't attend classes—though I'd like to eventually—but work privately with my professor. I am studying the relationship between culture and society, specifically the end of the 19th and beginning of the 20th century, the time of Schoenberg, Klimt, Kokoschka, Munch. I love to study! Of course, I also love to learn new music, to rehearse, to play, to perform, but there is a limit—I have to keep a balanced life to stay healthy. I cook a lot, I like to go to museums, go out with friends, and

I want to be around for my brother [Ryu, then a child and budding violinist also taught by their mother].

And now there is your foundation, Midori and Friends.

Yes, I established it about three years ago, and I'm very much involved with it. My idea was to inspire children through music, not necessarily to play, but to learn about different cultures and the communication between them, the discipline of concentrating and of dedicating yourself to something you love very much. I've always loved children and felt very close to them; just to be with them gives me so much energy! In the public schools today, music education virtually does not exist, and we try to provide the music. This year, the foundation is presenting more than 100 concerts in the public schools of New York City.

Jack Mitchell

How do you select the schools?

They apply to us. We choose 20 to 25 according to need and geographic location, and we also look for cooperation from the teachers; we really can't do anything without that. Each school gets five concerts a year. This year, it was one from me or one from [pianist] Emanuel Ax, and we also have a wonderful young string quartet called the Maia Quartet, a woodwind quintet, a brass group, and a jazz group; they each visit the schools. There are usually about 300 kids in the audience, grades three to five or six to eight. We also provide cassettes and videotapes for them to preview, and my office conducts teacher-orientation workshops beforehand. But the children don't just listen. We give them workbooks in which they keep a journal; they write down what they know about classical music, what they expect to hear at the concert, and their reactions to it. We all have themes for our programs: for example, I did a little world tour with music, and Manny Ax played composers associated with Paris. For that program, we talked extensively about Impressionism in the workbooks; in some schools, the art teachers had the students paint or draw in that style. So they are actually doing some work; they learn about different kinds of music, different instruments. We try to tie music to every aspect of education.

Midori's work in educating children about music is growing in its role in her career.

How do you find them as an audience?

I like them very, very much. They are so outgoing, so forward in their responses and in expressing their thoughts when I talk to them. They often write me letters afterward.

Recordings

Bach: Concerto for Two Violins and Orchestra, BWV 1043; Vivaldi: Concertos for Two Violins and Orchestra. Saint Paul Chamber Orchestra, Pinchas Zukerman, violinist and cond. (Philips 416389).

Bartók: Concertos Nos. 1 and 2. Berlin Philharmonic, Zubin Mehta, cond. (Sony Classical 45941).

Bruch: Scottish Fantasy; Sibelius: Concerto. Israel Philharmonic Orchestra, Zubin Mehta, cond. (Sony Classical 58967).

Elgar: Sonata in E Minor; Franck: Sonata in A Major. With Robert McDonald, piano (Sony Classical 63331).

Encore!: Music of Kreisler, Paganini, Tchaikovsky, and others. With Robert McDonald, piano (Sony Classical 52568).

Live at Carnegie Hall: Music of Beethoven, Strauss, Chopin, Liszt, Debussy, Ravel. With Robert McDonald, piano (Sony Classical 46742).

Paganini: 24 Caprices for Solo Violin, Op. 1 (CBS MK 44944).

Paganini: Concerto No. 1, Op. 6; Tchaikovsky: Sérénade mélancolique, Valse-Scherzo. Saint Louis Symphony Orchestra, Leonard Slatkin, cond. (Philips 420943).

Sibelius: Concerto. Israel Philharmonic Orchestra, Zubin Mehta, cond. (Sony Classical 58967).

Tchaikovsky: Concerto in D Major; Shostokovich: Concerto No. 1. Berlin Philharmonic, Claudio Abbado, cond. (Sony Classical 68338).

How is all this financed?

We fund-raise, among other things, and we also receive in-kind donations.

What other plans do you have for the immediate future?

Well, first of all, I'm going to Marlboro this summer for the entire eight weeks. It will be the first time I'll have so much experience playing chamber music, and I am just so happy, so excited, I look forward to it so much! I have to choose six works to play, but I haven't decided on them yet, because I want to be very careful. I'd love to do Schoenberg, Shostakovich, quartets by Beethoven, Mozart, Haydn, Debussy, Grieg; quintets by Mozart and Brahms, some Dvořák, also Smetana. . . .

That's a lot more than six! [Laughter.] And what are your plans for after the summer?

Well, of course I plan to play concerts and to continue my work with the foundation, but also to study and develop myself, and really to enjoy life.

Isaac Stern

Isaac Stern is one of the premiere violinists of the 20th century. With an illustrious worldwide stage career, more than 100 recordings, and countless premieres to his credit, he is known to every lover of the classical violin. His influence will last far beyond his own career, however, because of his work as guide and mentor to younger artists, many of whom are among the best of today's players. In this 1994 interview, Stern discusses his views on spotting and nurturing musical talent—as well as the role music has played in his own life.

Stern Talk

Edith Eisler

Walking into the sunny, spacious apartment overlooking New York's Central Park that Isaac Stern uses as his studio-office is like stepping into a picture gallery. Covering the walls from floor to ceiling is a photographic history of his life, showing him with all those who have been his collaborators on the concert stage and the world stage— a veritable *Who's Who* of the illustrious figures of the last half century. Then suddenly, among the familiar faces, those of his grandchildren smile at you. On the mantle stand his medals and awards from America, France, and Israel, among them the golden Oscar he received for the film *From Mao to Mozart: Isaac Stern in China.*

His name is a household word, but he is especially beloved by New Yorkers for his decisive role in saving Carnegie Hall from developers and the wreckers' ball. He speaks about that time with pride and enthusiasm: "It was in my apartment that it all began in January 1960, and by June I had help from friends and colleagues everywhere." A Citizens' Committee was formed, political figures of all persuasions participated in the negotiations, but, as expressed in a document inscribed by the Municipal Arts Society of New York, it was to Stern's "clear vision and persistence that we owe the preservation of a heritage."

Spanning nearly 60 years, Stern's extraordinary career has taken him all over the world as soloist and chamber-music player, as cultural goodwill ambassador, and also as discoverer, guide, and nurturer of young talents. Born in Russia in 1920, he came to San Francisco when he was ten months old. He started playing the violin at the age of eight; his principal teacher was Naoum Blinder, the concertmaster of the San Francisco Symphony. Following his debut in that city, he played in New York's Town Hall in 1937, then in Carnegie Hall in 1943. I heard him there shortly afterward; having arrived in this country in 1945, I was eager to hear as many American violinists as possible and was immediately captivated and enormously impressed by his playing. Since then, his tireless efforts on behalf of humanity have added a new dimension to a loyal fan's admiration. In this I know I am not alone, but I felt singularly privileged to have the opportunity of talking with him about his manifold activities and achievements and the connections between them. He smiled at my first question, "How do you find the time and energy for all the things you do?" and answered, "You know, I've asked myself that many times."

Henry Grossman

Isaac Stern has recently written (with Chaim Potok) an autobiography entitled *My First 79 Years* (Knopf, 1999).

With a flourishing virtuoso career that would have been enough for most performers, how did you get into playing so much chamber music?

Chamber music was always part of my life. In fact, I never "got into" anything: everything came to me. I didn't ask for anything, ever, ever. All I did was learn to play music. If you are looking for the connection between the things I do, you've found it: music.

And why differentiate between solo and chamber music? Chamber music is the basis of all music. I grew up playing it; it always was and has remained a very natural, joyous form of expression for me. When I was studying in San Francisco as a teenager, I played chamber music two or three times a week with the leading musicians of the city. The concertmaster of the Symphony was my teacher and all the first-chair players were my friends.

When I was about 15, I first heard the Budapest String Quartet, then the Pro Arte Quartet and the Stradivarius Quartet, so playing chamber music, for me, is not a different life than being a soloist. It is not a lesser life, it is not a less glamorous life, it is simply life. But there was a period when chamber music was not very fashionable, especially among young people. There were the concerts by the famous trio Heifetz-Rubinstein-Piatigorsky, but they were big stars getting together only occasionally. And the Casals-Cortot-Thibaut trio played mostly in Europe. Now, [pianist] Eugene Istomin, [cellist] Leonard Rose, and I were friends and made music for our pleasure, for fun. One day we said, "Why don't we do this a little more?" and that was the beginning

Please Accept a FREE issue of STRINGS Magazine

We hope you enjoy the diversity of information, insight, and wisdom in this book. This and material just like it appears in every issue of *Strings* Magazine.

If you're not already a subscriber to *Strings*, we'd like to send you the latest issue absolutely *FREE* in thanks for purchasing this book. Simply fill out this Free Issue Card and return it to us today.

Name _____ 493

Address _____

City _____ State ___ Zip ___

Country _____

Phone _____ E-mail _____

Please allow 4–6 weeks for delivery.

BUSINESS REPLY MAIL
FIRST-CLASS MAIL PERMIT NO. 99020 ESCONDIDO CA

POSTAGE WILL BE PAID BY ADDRESSEE

STRINGS

PO BOX 469020
ESCONDIDO CA 92046-9570

of our trio. You know the results; they were exciting and it was wonderful for all of us. We did a world tour with the complete chamber music of Beethoven—all ten violin and piano sonatas, the cello sonatas, the trios. We were lucky, because Eugene was one of the rarest musicians: he plays the piano like a stringed instrument, and Leonard and I had a very similar physical approach to the instrument in terms of bow speed, vibrato, and all that. And besides, we were friends. So it was a marvelous, exciting time for us; we played with great pleasure and also had much success.

Two things were particularly important. We made a series of recordings of which I am very proud: Beethoven, Brahms, Schubert, and Mendelssohn; and, as a result of our trio, it became very popular and terribly chic in this country to play chamber music, and suddenly lots of young people began doing it.

I remember those wonderful concerts you called "Isaac Stern and Friends" at Carnegie Hall.

Yes, that also became a popular title. Of course, when children are filled with certain unhealthy goals and ideas much too soon by ambitious teachers and parents, they don't realize that you not only have to learn how to play, but why to play—that's the most important thing. I find, even today, with some of the young hotshots who come and play up and down the fiddle in their virtuoso concertos—Paganini, Wieniawski, Tchaikovsky—that I have to slow them down and say, "When was the last time you played chamber music?" Everybody makes a stab at it, but not seriously enough. Again, the question is how you go into it and why.

You've contributed significantly to fostering a healthy attitude in your teaching and coaching. Will you tell me something about it?

I don't consider myself a teacher, really, because I've never worked with one student on a regular basis. I've heard many, many young people; many of those who have a career going now I've heard at some time, and I've made suggestions to them. I never did it in an organized way until my association with the Jerusalem Music Center, which was created in 1975.

I started with the young Israelis and young Russians and others who were coming there. I would be there for four or five days or a week, and I would hear a group of people several times, giving what they call master classes. That's an expression I dislike, because when you listen to people, you have to take them apart, but then you have to be there to put them back together. So my definition of a master class is having the time and patience to undo the damage you did in the first place. But that may take six months; in six days or one day, all you can have is an encounter, and sometimes a very brief encounter. Well, I got accustomed to these encounters, and I had a knack with young people and

What he plays

Isaac Stern currently plays on a Giuseppe Guarneri del Gesù violin known as the "Ysaÿe," made in Cremona in 1740. His favorite bows are a Tourte and a Pajeot. He uses various brands of metal strings.

Recordings

Isaac Stern's long career has resulted in a vast discography. One of the best introductions to his playing is Sony's multidisc set of recordings sold separately but collectively entitled Isaac Stern: A Life in Music. *Everything is there—concertos, sonatas, and a huge selection of chamber music, chosen from different decades. The list below is just a sampling of the pieces included in that set, which includes several dozen discs.*

Beethoven: Complete Sonatas for Piano and Violin. With Eugene Istomin, piano (Sony 64524).

Brahms: Quartet No. 1 in G Minor, Op. 25; No. 2 in A, Op. 26; No. 3 in C Minor, Op. 60. With Jaime Laredo, viola; Yo-Yo Ma, cello; Emanuel Ax, piano. Brahms: Trio No. 1 in B, Op. 8; No. 2 in C, Op. 87; No. 3 in C Minor, Op. 101. With Leonard Rose, cello; Eugene Istomin, piano (Sony 64520).

Mozart: Concertos. With the Cleveland Orchestra, George Szell, cond. (Sony 66475).

Mozart: Sonatas for Violin and Piano, K. 296, K. 454, K. 526. With Yefim Bronfman, piano (Sony 53972).

found that in listening to them, I could generally focus on the center of a problem, whether physical or musical or a combination of the two.

Then came the idea to have a two-week seminar on the chamber music of Beethoven and Brahms at Carnegie Hall, which was very successful, and I did a similar four-week seminar in Jerusalem immediately afterward. I've never wanted to be connected with a major musical institution, because that means having to accept existing standards already set by others. Also, there are friends and colleagues involved, and you don't want to get into discussions of who knows better what to do. It's much easier and more pleasant to keep things private and human between friends.

I heard your Carnegie Hall workshop in 1993. It was very interesting, the structure of having several coaches, sometimes more than students in the group, was quite new to me.

That was an experiment. It was very healthy for the ego, because you don't impose only one person's ego on the students. I think the basic idea was sound, but you have to control the numbers: if there are more than three coaches, it can be bad, because you begin to talk among yourselves. Also, I wanted the players to perform, not the teachers. I never touched the violin, except perhaps to demonstrate a vibrato, or a better way to hold the instrument or the bow. The students have to learn to use their own brains, to realize themselves what they are doing. I worked with them very, very intensely. [Editor's note: The workshops have continued throughout the 1990s and moved well past the "experimental" stage.]

Henry Grossman

Stern has earned his recognition as both a soloist and a chamber-music player.

How did you select the groups?

Other people picked them; I chose out of the final group from video-tapes and audiocassettes.

And how did you choose your colleagues?

They are people with whom I've played chamber music and shared other musical experiences.

Though you heard each group several times, how much good do you think one can do on such a short-term basis?

I have no idea. I try it, and often I am more pleased by the results than I thought possible. You can do a lot of harm, but you can also do a lot of good.

You also do a lot of good in other ways—for example, by discovering a lot of young talents. How do you find them?

People come and play for me, colleagues tell me about them, people talk. There is a very well-developed underground system among artists.

I've always been grateful for the opportunities music gave me for a good life, so I feel I've got to give something back. And the best way to do that is through young people. Being with and around them keeps you young, and it is lovely to see young people become people, which is really the whole name of the game.

How do you spot a superior talent?

It's something you learn to recognize. I can feel it, because I've been around, I know what it takes to be a performer. I am one myself, and I think about the way I play and the way other people play. What interests me is the kind of playing that does not ask, but demands that people listen, and I can identify that right away. It has nothing to do with age: I heard Sarah Chang when she was six or seven, Midori when she was nine, Itzhak Perlman and Pinchas Zukerman when they were ten or 11, Yo-Yo Ma when he was six or seven, Yefim Bronfman when he was 15 or 16, and with all of them I could tell right away what sort of talents they were. Now what goes on in my head, how I reach a conclusion—that I cannot tell you or anybody else. It's mine to know, it's within my own psyche, it's based on my life. All of us react to some degree in the mirror of our own minds.

But not everybody can or will do as much as you for their protégés.

All I do is listen and try to guide, encourage the young people to become personalities in their own image, not somebody else's, within the limits of the music. I do not sponsor, I do not push; I cannot invent a manager or create a career. I have no magic wand—such a thing does not exist.

Many of those you just mentioned were prodigies. How do you feel about that?

I have some pity for them, but the history of prodigies goes back 300 years. There was one named Mozart.

Might he not have lived longer if he had not been a prodigy?

I don't think so; it had more to do with the society in which he lived. Another prodigy was Mendelssohn, who wrote the Octet at the age of 16. Creative prodigies sometimes burn out; it's happened many times in mathematics and the sciences. What do you think a prodigy is?

I think a prodigy is like a hothouse plant that's been forced to bloom prematurely.

I disagree with you. I think a true prodigy is someone who has intuitions and perceptions that other people don't have. There's no normalcy for real prodigies, because they are by definition outside the norm—that's what makes them prodigies. Theirs is a talent that has to be guided, not crushed; respected, not pushed.

But they are pushed, aren't they? They are robbed of their childhood by being driven to achieve.

That's because much of the time it's a passport out of the ghetto for their parents. It happened to the Jews in the 19th century, and it's exactly the same thing now, although it may be a mental, psychological, or economic ghetto they are trying to get out of.

At the expense of their children?

That's never stopped people before. And that's not how they see it: parents want a better life for their children, otherwise the United States would never have been created as a country.

So what happens to performing prodigies who learn to play great music with their fingers long before their heads and hearts are ready for it?

That's their problem. To be a performer, you must learn to look at yourself with more honesty and cruelty, and less pity, than anybody else would. Some grow into it very well. Every person of extraordinary talent I've known was in that category: Rachmaninoff, Rubinstein, Schnabel, Kreisler, Heifetz, Piatigorsky, Szell, Monteux, Munch, Reiner, Ormandy. But we must remember that they lived in a time completely different from ours. You couldn't fly around the world in three hours; you didn't have endless seasons playing nine months out of the year; you didn't have television or good recordings. So they had more time to mature, to study, even to rest.

There is no comparison between the structure of musical life today and when I grew up. I've been a performer now for almost 60 years— that's a long time. Think of how many wrong notes have passed under my bridge!

I'm thinking of all the music that has flowed and is still flowing out of your fiddle. When do you find time to practice?

I practice very hard to this day. You do it when you have to, and it's lovely to work and concentrate. I like to do it very late at night; I am not a morning person.

And your plans for the future?

To live long and enjoy it.

Corey Cerovsek

*Corey Cerovsek, with some dozen years of worldwide perfor-
mances behind him, is still among the younger of today's top violinists; he will be only 28 when the century turns. But, as is clear
in this 1997 interview, he is making a name for himself in the
quiet, understated manner of a talent that puts the music first and
publicity second—although his public appearances include performances on* The Tonight Show *as well as at London's Wigmore
Hall. While his discography is still in its early stages, Cerovsek
promises to last well into the 21st century as a favorite among
lovers of the violin.*

A Perfect Harmony

Timothy Pfaff

It's not every violinist who scales the summit of the Alban Berg
Concerto—or who even cares to. Seldom technically flashy and, violinists say, only intermittently difficult to execute, the Berg is not a fiddler's piece. It appeals to a certain kind of musician, one of a thoughtful, questing cast of mind. Corey Cerovsek plays it as though it were
written for him.

When the famously risk-taking conductor Michael Tilson Thomas
announced Cerovsek as his soloist in the Berg for the San Francisco
Symphony's "Celebrations of the Sacred and Profane: Music of Heaven
and Earth" festival in June 1997, savvy orchestra watchers snapped to
attention. What were the odds that a little-known, 25-year-old
Canadian was up to the task? The last violinist from the under-30 crowd
to make a mark on the work (an indelible one, as it turned out, in a
Chicago Symphony Orchestra subscription series conducted by Pierre
Boulez) was the phenomenal, and to all intents ageless, Midori. Who
was this Corey Cerovsek?

After his two SFS festival performances of the Berg, both of which were completely assured, interpretively engaged and engaging, and so relaxed and spontaneous that they were appreciably different in that "in the moment" way, San Francisco audiences learned what their counterparts around the world already knew: Corey Cerovsek isn't just a young violinist to watch, he's one to listen to—and savor—now.

"I don't play anything else that compares to the Berg in emotional depth," Cerovsek says in an impromptu interview in his hotel room between the performances. "Even though I've spent more time looking at this piece, from the standpoint of how it's put together, than I have at anything else I play, I still don't feel that I know every facet of it. You learn a lot performing any piece, but that's particularly true with the Berg. I know I'm lucky to have had a chance to have played it quite a few times. It has a special place in my repertoire."

J. Henry Fair

The Berg is one of Corey Cerovsek's favorite concertos.

Berg's 1935 masterpiece and last completed composition—to many minds the only true justification or consolation for the composer's consequent inability to complete the orchestration on his great second opera, *Lulu*—draws a particular strain of interpreter. The intellectual rigor of its architecture, the depth of its emotion, and the yearning arc of its elegiac spirit together select the piece's interpreters.

Cerovsek's critically acclaimed performances of the work in San Francisco confirmed his place among the concerto's elect. Cerovsek's complete grasp of the work's long, complex span—a grasp remarkable in a player of any age, to say nothing of one 25—made the half-hour concerto feel like it lasted a mere instant.

"It is fascinating what this piece does to your sense of time," Cerovsek allowed. "It's particularly true when you're playing it. Aside from the space between the Chorale statement in the last movement [in which Berg quotes the chorale "Es ist genug" from Bach's cantata *O Ewigkeit, du Donnerwort*] and the variations that bring it to a close— that's the longest tutti, just 12 or 16 bars—there isn't much time when the solo violin isn't playing. The piece isn't in a rigorous, traditional sonata-allegro. Its form seems spontaneous, yet it is highly structured. There's no excess, no fat, and the transitions from section to section are entirely natural, so much so that you don't even feel them as transitions. The whole piece flows from beginning to end as one unit.

"It's wonderfully written," Cerovsek continues. "Nothing about it seems arbitrary. The intervals feel very violinistic, and the piece fits very comfortably in the hand. It feels right. In other concertos there are those passages where you find yourself asking, 'Why is it written like this, and do I really have to play it?' There's nothing like that in the Berg.

"I don't call this music atonal, even though to some people it is, at least theoretically. Perhaps that's because the row is jerry-rigged to be pseudotonal. In any case, there's a lot of implied harmony. When it's dissonant, or difficult harmonically, it can sound angry. I don't know if that response is an innate, physiological thing or something culturally inherited. But given that, I find the humorous, more spirited moments—the *Ländler* sections and scherzando passages of the first movement—a good contrast. Those passages have to be done with a certain spirit, and I'm still experimenting with them.

"There are certain pieces that give you deep aesthetic pleasure, both from how they're put together and what they ultimately achieve. This piece is clearly one of them. I'll be depressed when I finish these performances because I don't have another Berg on my calendar. And for the next few days—when I should be thinking about other repertoire—when I let my brain go, I'll be thinking about the Berg. It's hard to get it out of your system."

Cerovsek's first exposure to the Berg also came at the invitation of Tilson Thomas, who invited the young violinist to play the piece with the conductor's Miami-based New World Symphony. Between then and the San Francisco reprises with the conductor, which brought his total number of performances of the concerto to a dozen, Cerovsek has played it on a tour of Denmark with the Tivoli Orchestra and with the orchestra of the Spanish province of Asturias.

"The Miami performances came during a very busy period in my schedule," Cerovsek recalls, "so I didn't even have a chance to go through it with piano before the first rehearsal. But I had put in an unusually large amount of time studying the piece. It had come up more than once in my music courses at Indiana University. As a result, I knew in the abstract how it was put together long before I knew what was going on inside it, at the gut level. I just winged it—wung it? What's the past tense of that?

"I like to take risks like that sometimes. Michael [Tilson Thomas] was very helpful. He knew I hadn't played the piece and he wanted to break me in with it, and he certainly has ideas about how it should go. And the young people in that orchestra are very bright, very good players. The whole thing came out really nicely. I have to admit, the first time you play the Berg, you're concerned about playing the right notes in the right places. Once that ceases to be a worry—once you know where everything is, and you feel at home—you can relax and start playing with the music. Alongside its sublime and serious passages are some wonderfully playful, seductive, tongue-in-cheek moments, so there's lots to play with.

"The other entertaining thing about that experience," he adds with almost indecent if genuine nonchalance, "is that before it started I found out there was a music critics' convention in town. There were 45 critics at that concert. I decided not to tell my parents about that, knowing full well that they would freak out on my behalf."

What he plays

Corey Cerovsek currently plays a Guarneri del Gesù violin made in Cremona in 1742. On loan to him through the Stradivari Society of Chicago, the instrument is the one owned by Henryk Wieniawski at the end of his life. Earlier, Cerovsek played the "ex-Sennhauser" del Gesù, made in Cremona in 1735 and also on loan through the Stradivari Society. What began as a short-term loan of the Wieniawski instrument has become a longer-term arrangement.

"Both of the instruments are great," Cerovsek says. "In my view, what makes a violin great is its ability to give you a sense that it moves in sympathy with your intentions. When I play the Wieniawski del Gesù, I find much more than a beautiful sound. The instrument has a soul.

"The instrument is powerful and confident on the G and E strings and soulful in the middle—where there is a wolf that is frustrating but also endearing—in a way that resonates with my own personality. The wolf points to a register of the instrument and tells me that near that point I have to play in a particularly human way: assertively, joyfully, throaty, and whispering by turns."

Before the loan of the first del Gesù, Cerovsek bought a Giovanni Francesco Pressenda violin, ca. 1839. "It's a nice instrument," he says, "but you just can't compare it with a del Gesù. It had a brilliant, projecting kind of soprano sound. The del Gesù is much darker, requiring less in the way of bow speed but considerably more digging in. The string length is a little shorter on the del Gesù, and it's slightly small. That's great for getting around, but it required some intonation calibration on my part. But it was worth it." Cerovsek now also has a 1908 Stefano Scarampella violin.

"I play most of my concerts with a [François] Voirin bow, and I've got a [Eugène] Sartory for backup. For strings I use Dominant G, D, and A and a Pirastro Wondertone E. I keep meaning to experiment with others, but there's never a good time to experiment with strings!"

Recordings

Corey Cerovsek Plays Wieniawski. With Katja Cerovsek, piano (Delos DE 3231).

Mozart: Adagios. With Carol Rosenberger, piano; Allan Vogel, oboe. Moscow Chamber Orchestra, Constantine Orbelian, cond. (Delos DE 3243).

Russian Soul: Music of Tchaikovsky, Gilère, Scriabin, Shostakovich, Borodin, and others. Moscow Chamber Orchestra, Constantine Orbelian, cond. (Delos DE 3244).

Cerovsek's animated yet down-to-earth, boy-next-door manner, free laugh, dancing eyes, and unruffled cordiality thinly belie a tireless mind that responds thoughtfully to a barrage of questions. Even the seemingly simple question of how he pronounces his name yields a complex response. "When I'm in the States, I say 'Sir-*off*-seck,' because it's just easier for everybody. It's that 'v' before the 's' that throws people. But my parents, who are Austrian, say '*Tsehr*-off-seck.' We don't actually know enough about the family history to know what kind of name it is, beyond that it's obviously Austro-Hungarian. Some people think it's Czech, but it seems more likely it's Slovenian, or perhaps Croatian."

Although neither of Cerovsek's parents is particularly musical— his mother is an amateur singer, his father a structural engineer—the couple raised a pair of musical offspring. Cerovsek has performed regularly with his older sister, Katja, an accomplished pianist and, since the two know each other so well, something of an ideal musical partner.

"When my parents moved to Canada from Austria, they bought an upright piano before they got any other furniture. And they took my sister and me to symphony concerts from a very young age. My mother took singing lessons and my sister took piano lessons, so it was just natural for me to climb up on the piano bench and try to play. Eventually, I also started taking piano lessons, but I had problems with my first teacher. She made me keep playing a piece called 'The Little Roguish Clown,' which I detested. I think I was ready for something more challenging.

"Luckily, my parents recognized that I loved music," he continues. "Soon after I put the piano on pause, they spotted a quarter-size violin in a shop window and bought it for me for Christmas, when I was six. It was spooky. I don't remember asking for a violin, but it was love at first sight. They actually have a videotape of me running around the house screaming, 'I got a violin from Santa!' Apparently within weeks I was telling everyone I was going to be a violinist when I grew up. Somehow that wish never went away, and it magically turned into reality without my knowing when it crossed that boundary."

Were there any doubt that Cerovsek is a natural musician, the saga of his return to the piano would neatly eliminate it. After "stealing some piano lessons from my sister's teachers," Cerovsek made a serious return to the instrument when the family moved to Bloomington, Indiana, when he was 12, expressly so that he could begin his studies with the legendary violinist and teacher Josef Gingold. After some provisional piano lessons with a student assistant, he resumed study with a member of Indiana's piano faculty who acknowledged his gifts as a violinist but gently urged him to think about continuing with the piano, too.

Cerovsek did more than think about it. "I started performing on piano about ten years ago. The Palo Alto Chamber Orchestra, a youth orchestra in California, asked me to tour Australia with them, mostly playing violin: *The Four Seasons* and the Mozart A-Major Concerto.

Then somebody got the idea it would be fun if I played piano, too. Because the situation was pretty low-key, I also played Mozart's 'Jeunehomme' [Piano] Concerto on the tour. Since then I've played concertos on both instruments a number of times. Next month [July 1997], I'll be playing the Sibelius Violin Concerto and the Mozart C-Major Piano Concerto, K. 467, at a festival in Montpellier, France.

"I don't advertise that I do this, but secretly I like to be forced to do it once in a while," he admits. "The rest of the time I complain, because it's so hard to find good pianos to practice on, especially when you're touring as a violinist."

J. Henry Fair

Footage of a Cerovsek piano performance (another Mozart concerto) in a television interview that aired on *CBS Sunday Morning* in 1997 gives ample evidence of an accomplished, stylish, and persuasive Mozart pianist playing with the trademark fluency and relaxation Cerovsek brings to his concerts on violin.

"I wouldn't claim to be as good a pianist as I hope to be a violinist," he counters. "But it's good to have another musical perspective. Performing on the piano is informative, because it forces me to think differently, musically. On the violin you have the luxury of shaping the sound a great deal

Cerovsek's similar age and training have brought comparisons with Joshua Bell.

after you start the note. On the piano, you've got to think ahead and plan out your phrasing, your attacks, and the articulation.

"The philosophy I apply to both instruments is to stick to basic principles: avoid tension and find the path of least resistance. These principles apply to either instrument and guarantee a certain degree of success. That and youth, of course, which will only last so long. Mr. Gingold, with whom I studied the most, was never a stickler for a particular technique. He endorsed the rather unorthodox philosophy of doing what works for you, within bounds of rationality, of course."

Cerovsek's decade of active study with Gingold led to sometimes tryingly regular comparisons with another famous Gingold protégé, Joshua Bell. "I remember once walking into the graduate office at Bloomington," he recalls, "and having the secretary greet me with, 'You must be Corey Bell.' I'm getting used to it. In one respect, it's not surprising. Josh and I use some of the same vocabulary—certain kinds of shifting, certain qualities of sound—that we got from Gingold. But we deploy them differently, and somehow we end up going in completely different directions. Thank God Josh is a lot of fun. We tend to run into each other a couple times a year, in one place or another.

"I think it's a credit to Mr. Gingold that his students do come out completely different. He didn't impose himself on his students. That said, I don't think there's much about my playing that wasn't affected by him. He loved holding the instrument, the sensation of playing each note. One of the things all his students inherited from him is his attitude. He was in love with the violin, and with being a violinist and a musician. Sometimes I'm envious of the fact that he came from a generation when it was—or it seems now that it was—easier to be completely absorbed in that. Culturally, classical music is less prominent now, and the modern world has become more complicated. I can't claim to have his violin-is-all-there-is-to-life attitude, but it was a wonderful thing to see. It was like looking at a couple and thinking, 'See how in love they are.'

"Mr. Gingold's playing was unabashedly old-fashioned. He was the master of the golden sound—and the slides and all those other stylistic traits that go along with it. He thoroughly enjoyed a part of the repertoire that has partially gone out of fashion: the fiddle music. I'm proud to consider that stuff a part of my repertoire, too. I wouldn't be happy with it as a steady diet, but you can have a blend of the sublime—the Beethoven Concerto, say, or the Brahms—and these wonderful character pieces. For me, life wouldn't be complete without both.

"The most important thing for Gingold, always, was to enjoy playing," Cerovsek adds. "So now I try not to run myself to the wall and torture myself with work. I regularly ask myself if I'm enjoying myself, if I feel fulfilled. That's important for your mental health as a performer."

Despite a rapidly burgeoning career as orchestra soloist and recitalist that is taking him to increasingly more prominent orchestras and festivals—and rarely returning him to his own home in Bloomington—Cerovsek seems the picture of performer's mental health. He insists that his biggest stage fright came while playing a jury recital at Bloomington ("having the whole faculty there, including [cellist Janos] Starker and [pianist Menahem] Pressler, made an impression on me"). When it does come, he says, "the music sweeps it away in a minute or two."

Asked about his memory, he answers without hesitation, "Good, frankly. It's not at all photographic, though. I joke that it's photographic but blurry. Sometimes my fingers memorize a piece before my brain does, but I don't like the sensation of playing something but not knowing what or why. What buttresses memory is taking the time to see how a piece is put together. A long-range sense of where things are going trickles down into the details, and that makes memory a lot easier. I'm impulsive, but always with the brain on. I don't spend long stretches of music in a complete trance. There's a supervisor back there who's watching what's going on.

"Not all of my repertoire is available overnight—but half of it is. Give me a day, and it will be back. As a result, I'm crazily willing to do almost anything on short notice. This season [1997] I've done a whole series of cancellations. In April I filled in for Nadja [Salerno-Sonnenberg] in Detroit with the Brahms. I ended up with this bizarre schedule during which I played Wednesday night in Palm Beach, a recital in Toronto Thursday, and Brahms in Detroit Friday morning—with no way to get there. I had to get someone to drive me through the night from Toronto to Detroit to play Brahms in the morning—morning Brahms!—on four hours' sleep. I don't like putting tails on in the morning. My management just called to say that Philadelphia needs someone to play Dvořák, and I'm proud that this time I said no. I've done 12 different concertos in the last eight weeks. There's only so much you can do."

For Cerovsek, that realization has extended to fundamental career choices. The simple if astonishing fact is that his career in music has come at the expense of an equally promising career in mathematics. While studying with Gingold and enrolled at Indiana University, Cerovsek completed his bachelor's degree in music and math at age 15, his master's degree in both the following year, and doctoral course work in both by the time he was 18. "The longer I go on being this busy playing," he observes, "the less likely it is I'm going to withdraw from public life to write a dissertation or two. It's a shame to see all those credit hours go to waste, but it doesn't seem all that, well, useful.

J. Henry Fair

"But math remains a big part of my personality and my mental life, and it provides a kind of restful oasis from the general zaniness of being a musician. It's like a hobby-plus. I love to read in the sciences, especially theoretical physics, and if you see me out talking a walk and just sort of staring off, I'm probably thinking about the nature of space and time."

Cerovsek's academic degrees include mathematics as well as music.

Cerovsek recognizes that aptitudes for music and math are often paired. "They do seem to go together," he reflects, "though, statistically, I think there are more mathematicians and scientists who enjoy music as a sideline than people who make music and have math on the side. But in my case that's because I'm impractical and governed by my emotions for the violin," he adds with a gently self-mocking laugh.

"There's no question that a central aspect of my playing is always going to be rational. I'm not comfortable if I can't answer the question: 'If I were composing this piece, why would I put the various elements where they are?' That's just part of my personality. But there's also no question that my emotional response to music is instinctive. I never try to rationalize why I feel a certain thing where I do. One of the reasons I perform—and can't imagine not performing—is because so many of the feelings that are difficult to process in real life come out so easily and so well in music. It's cathartic for me to play.

"I'm not a particularly demonstrative or exhibitionist player, but I have no shame emotionally when it comes to playing. It's wonderful to have an arena where you can let yourself go completely. I stop worrying, because there's the safety that you can say things much more deeply than you could as a person in so-called normal life.

"Sometimes there's a slightly plaintive voice in the back of my head that tells me if I had applied myself to math, I could work for some software company for millions of dollars and could buy myself the del Gesù I play. It's crass, all of it, but it is in the back of my head. I don't want my brain to atrophy, so I keep the scientific side up for my own interest. And there's this practical, techno streak in me that means that I always travel with a laptop and love hooking up to e-mail and checking my faxes at home from the road. We musicians do these things because we can't help ourselves.

"I've had people in the graduate math department tell me they don't understand why I'm doing this music thing, and it breaks my heart. On one hand, there are these one-way choices we make. But on the other, I think these things we know apply more fluidly than we often think. I like to know about a lot of things, and I sincerely believe that the more you add to the pot, the better the stew. I may not be applying my math skills to my career directly, but I think they're back there working anyway—particularly when playing a piece like the Berg, which has a very complicated set of interrelationships, many of them mathematical. Bad as it has sometimes felt to leave the math career behind, I got swept away with the music, and I know I wouldn't be happy the other way around."

Nadja Salerno-Sonnenberg

Nadja Salerno-Sonnenberg, a highly talented soloist with great audience appeal, encountered her biggest professional problem in 1994 in her own kitchen. On Christmas day, while cooking, she accidentally sliced off the tip of the little finger of her left hand. Surgeons managed to repair the finger, but her recovery involved months of healing and rehabilitation at the physical, emotional, and musical levels.

Since then, however, Salerno-Sonnenberg has returned to the stage with all her old vitality—and perhaps more. She is busy performing and recording, and in 1999 she was awarded the Avery Fisher Prize for musical excellence. This interview, held shortly before her injury, provides a look at the artist before she had to deal with a frighteningly real threat to her career and her most treasured means of self-expression.

Risky Business

Todd Brewster

Since she won the international Naumburg prize in 1981 and left Juilliard and teacher Dorothy DeLay to pursue a solo career, violinist Nadja Salerno-Sonnenberg has been that rarest of American citizens: a classical musician with a mainstream popular following. Much of that popularity, charge her many critics, is the work of a clever press agency capitalizing on the musician's vivacious personality. After all, this is no

ordinary virtuoso. Salerno-Sonnenberg laughs, smokes, and, in performance, gyrates her body to the rhythm of the orchestral tutti. She favors
stunning clothes and dresses her recordings up with provocative (for
classical music, at any rate) photographs. CBS' *60 Minutes* has profiled
her; Johnny Carson had her on his program six times; and, fulfilling
what she described as a lifelong dream, Salerno-Sonnenberg was once
photographed for a magazine dressed in pinstripes, fiddle in hand, on
the field at Yankee Stadium.

But hype dies young and, having established herself with such fan-
fare, Salerno-Sonnenberg, at 33, is today facing a more dramatic challenge: staying on top. While praising her vivid stage presence, many
reviewers continue to describe hers as a career built primarily on
celebrity. The *New York Times,* whose chief critic once referred to her as
only "moderately gifted," panned Salerno-Sonnenberg's performance of
the Bruch concerto with the New York Philharmonic [in early 1994].
But the artist remains nonplussed. She rejects the notion that her career
was manufactured, describes her devotion to a performance ethic built
on "risk taking," and demonstrates an unshakable confidence in her
musicianship. And why not? Critical pans notwithstanding, Salerno-
Sonnenberg's recent recording of encore favorites, *It Ain't Necessarily So*
(EMI CDC-54314), has proven to be one of the hottest-selling classical
albums in recent years.

*Your career began with an avalanche of press, both positive and negative.
Did you find that difficult?*

When you experience that kind of attention it is mind-boggling, but
things have calmed down now. I simply had no idea that the press
would take off like a snowball on the fact that I enjoyed watching base-
ball! I never thought it was so interesting. But what happened was that
these reporters got ahold of certain facts—they're not lies—and then,
like anyone else, they interpreted those facts as they wished. If one
decent article was written, months later I would see a quote from the
same piece in another city. You could never get away from it. So you get
used to it. I do the things that people say I do. But for somebody to
interview you and then pretend that they know you and that they can
describe your entire approach to music simply because they've learned
a few facts about you, well, that is silly. But I feel calmer now because
I'm still here and time—longevity—is what it is all about.

Did the attention help you reach a larger audience?

It did. Particularly after I was on *60 Minutes.* I think in the beginning of
my career, people were curious; they wanted to know who I was. But
that's all over. At this point, anyone who comes to hear me play knows
me already, knows my playing. That's why I can be calm.

Was the publicity calculated? Did you and your manager sit down and map it all out?

No and no.

What about the photos on the album jackets?

Well, OK, that was calculated. But if it helps us sell more records, why shouldn't we go with interesting album jackets? Recognizing where classical music is these days and where it has to go in order to survive, I think things like attractive album jackets have become very important. It simply helps to sell the music, and I am all for using the media to sell classical music since I am a classical musician. But even if I wasn't, I'd hate to see the art form die. It's also fun. It's fun to match the album photo with the music so that the album covers give you an idea of what you will be listening to.

Bernard Vidal

But don't such tactics promote music for the wrong reasons?

Yes, that's true, but we have to promote classical music for both wrong and right reasons just to survive. The days when you could let the music sell itself are gone. I'm not just speaking about my career. I'm speaking very generally about the fact that if the cover said *It Ain't Necessarily So and Other Encores by Nadja Salerno-Sonnenberg* and had a picture of a tree, it wouldn't sell. You need something else to grab people.

This photo, used on the cover of *It Ain't Necessarily So,* caused a stir when the album came out.

Are these the kinds of people you want buying your album?

Who knows? All I can say is that I am particularly proud of that album. I even listen to it myself from time to time. And it's what I said before: a good example of matching the picture with the contents. The picture and the title of the album are supposed to suggest that what you see is not necessarily what you are going to get. So the juxtaposition of my outfit and the warehouse setting—well, it's provocative. I don't know what people expect, but it grabs their attention. As for people who know my playing, they couldn't care less about what kind of photo is on the jacket.

How do your colleagues react to this attitude?

Some might be turning their noses up, but I don't really know anything about that. I don't have that many close friends in the business. But I have noticed that an awful lot of other people are doing it now. I go into a record store and see plenty of recordings by very serious musicians, not flamboyant people, and their albums have these kinds of covers as well. And, of course, I don't find any problem with it.

What she plays

Salerno-Sonnenberg owns three violins. In 1993 she acquired a Pietro Guarneri of Venice from 1724; she also owns a violin built for her in 1974 by the East Coast maker Sergio Peresson. "I haven't heard all of them," she says, "but I think it's one of the best Peressons ever made. He was a personal friend of the family and he was one of the finest modern makers." Salerno-Sonnenberg's third violin is by an unknown maker, "but it is a cannon—it's loud!" she says. "It's very useful for certain repertoire, and it's fun! Right now I'm playing the Guarneri the most, but for repertoire where there's a lot going on and the orchestration is large and thick, I might use one of the others."

She uses Dominant strings and owns two bows, one by the contemporary maker John Norwood Lee of Chicago and one by the 19th-century Dutch bow maker Karel Van der Meer. "The Norwood Lee is a much heavier bow, the Van der Meer much lighter," she explains. "I would like to find something in between."

M.J. Quay

So let's change the subject. How have you grown musically?

My technique is better. I took it upon myself about four years ago to seriously try to correct the bad habits I developed as a student, things like incorrect shifting. I shift much better going up and not so well going down, and I had avoided using my pinky finger for most of my life. It's naturally the weakest finger and it wasn't one I relied on; I used it only when I had to. I've also been going back to basics—scales, open strings, anything to try to undo the wrong that was done. I have become far more serious about my own playing than I ever was before. I knew that I already had this big career and that keeping it was going to be harder than getting it. Just for my own feelings of self-worth, I wanted to be able to know that there wasn't anything I could not play. So I started a regimen to improve things.

What kind of technical regimen had you followed before?

Not much of one. I had a very good, basic training when I was very young, and then throughout my teens I developed some bad habits, either because I had been misguided or, as was more often the case, I was lazy. And then I realized much later on that there was nothing more important to me than playing the fiddle well. So I wanted to correct these things. Also, there were certain times when a passage was so difficult that I had to practice it more than I'm sure other violinists practiced it, and when that happened I'd ask myself why. It was confirmation that I was a violinist and that I wanted to be, corny as it may sound, the best that I could be. I have four good fingers and a good right arm just like anybody else. There's no reason for me not to be able to play anything.

Would you say, then, that you've matured? That you've become less of the maverick that you were when the press descended on you?

Well, yes and no. I became very, very serious about technique. Also along the way I learned many, many things about music in general, about making music, about working with an orchestra, what works, what doesn't work, the chances you can take, and the chances you shouldn't take. All of this adds up to making a more mature and confident musician. But that doesn't mean that my playing has calmed down, it's just my attitude about my playing. I don't feel desperate to prove something every time I walk on stage. What I want and what I get most of the time is a fully enjoyable experience. And that's combined with a lot of things, like cutting down on concerts so that I can be not only fully prepared but also full of energy.

How many concerts do you do a year now?

About 60, and no matter how many I cut out, I still feel I'm too busy.

How many of the 60 are you proud of?

There's always a passage here or there in any concert that you wish you had done better. Or you may be sick and your energy is only at 80 percent. But because I've cut down I can be not only completely prepared but eager to be on stage. These days, when I'm performing, there is nowhere else I'd rather be.

But of the 60, how many were you playing at the top of your form?

That's a different question. Now you're talking about playing in the zone. That's not just walking on stage and playing a very good performance, even a great performance, but walking on stage and feeling that if someone were to cut off both my arms I still would play great. That happens once or twice a year. Maybe.

Do you know why that happens when it happens?

No, and I don't think anybody does, but usually it's in a town you've never heard of. When it happens in New York—and sometimes it does happen in New York—well, then you think, "Wow!"

What music have you not played that you're dying to play?

For a long time it was the Sibelius Concerto, which I quite stupidly waited a long time to learn. I felt that I wasn't ready for the piece. It's technically very challenging, and I always felt it was for me, a piece absolutely written for me. But I kept putting off learning it until I felt I could do it justice. And I think that was stupid. I should have learned it when I was a teenager, a student. Because when I learned it, I was 28 and had already established who I was, and if I went to practice it for an hour and it didn't sound fabulous in an hour I had the extra burden of my ego saying, "Hey, whassamatter? I am so-and-so and I should be able to play this."

As for other repertoire, I'm dying to play the Walton Concerto. I'm trying to find time to learn it in hotel rooms here and there. I play the Bach solo sonatas and partitas every day but I have yet to program them. And to tell you the truth, I don't know why, but I suppose there is some fear there. The partitas are supremely difficult and are such masterworks that it's not enough to go on stage and play them. For me, I would want to put some stamp on the performance. Though I play them for myself, I feel a little trepidation about programming them, and I don't know when it will end.

Aren't there also some other reasons for learning music early? For instance, if you learn something when you're young, you can grow up with it.

Growing up with the piece is one way to put it. But the lesson I'm trying to impart is this: I think it's very important for a young person to learn the standard literature as early as possible, and, if possible, to get a performance of it somewhere, anywhere, any little dinky place, so that in their head they know that they've done it. Then, when they approach it later in life and their head is full of doubts, they can tell themselves that they've done it before.

Because when you play as a child you play without doubts?

Well, this is where prodigies are so incredible! They walk out on stage and play the most difficult repertoire, not only technically well but with some musicality and insight, and they don't know what they are doing! I didn't know what I was doing when I was ten or 12. When I walked on stage to play with the Philadelphia Orchestra when I was ten years old and there were 15,000 people in the audience, I wasn't nervous. I was concerned with not tripping over the wires because it was an outdoor concert, and that's about it. That and that my socks wouldn't fall down. You just don't think! Later in life, when I had to play the *Carmen Fantasie* with the Philadelphia, I realized, "This piece is hard and this is the Philadelphia Orchestra and I'm at the Academy of Music!"

Would you say, then, that performing is an art unto itself, that it is separate from musicianship?

I think it is for many people, but not for me. I have always, upon learning a piece, put my body

J. Henry Fair

Nadja Salerno-Sonnenberg is the subject of a prize-winning documentary, *Speaking in Strings*, which premiered at the 1999 Sundance Film Festival.

and mind into the situation of a performance. There have been times when I have been so nervous about an upcoming performance—perhaps a first performance of a new piece—that I have actually put make-up on, put on the outfit that I would wear on stage, walked into my dining room, taken a bow, and pretended to play the piece. I can actually envision the audience there, and to tell you the truth I get nervous enough that my bow shakes, and everything happens that can happen to you on stage. So, by the time I walk on stage literally, I've already done it. It's not a problem. I've never had stage fright. I was as nervous to perform the Sibelius Concerto in my dining room in preparation for my performance at Carnegie Hall as I was when I walked on stage at Carnegie.

This is with no one there in your living room but you?

No one. Just me. Listen, I don't do this all the time, but I know when I am going to need it. That's when I put myself in that mode. You know, there comes a time when you are as prepared as you can possibly be, in every way. The piece, the notes, technically. Your analysis of the piece. And your mind takes over and it's mind over matter at that point. You can tell yourself, for an upcoming difficult passage, that you're not going to get it, or you can do the reverse of that. I think any performer who performs a lot will agree with that. The mind takes over at a certain point and you've just got to believe that you can do it. You cannot doubt yourself on stage! It won't work no matter how prepared you are. I have seen great players completely fall apart on stage.

Anything like that ever happen to you?

No. Not that severe. But I'm the kind of person who always thinks tonight is the night that it will happen. I would never take it for granted that my mental powers would always be with me. I depend on them. I depend on my incredible ability to concentrate when I need to, which is when I am on stage. But I never take it for granted. I have seen young artists who can't handle playing on stage and I have seen older artists who have been on stage their entire lives who lose it. And it's so scary. That's the scariest thing in the world for me to see: an established artist who can't play for one reason or another. What has happened to me at concerts here and there is that I have become so distracted by personal things that I wasn't really there. Difficult to deal with, but it happens once in a blue moon.

Do you use any techniques to focus your concentration?

No. There's always a moment backstage before I walk on where I talk to myself. And when I am on stage the only thing I can say is that I try to block everything out and think so much of every single note in the piece that my mind becomes inundated with notes, with the music, with the passages, with what's coming up, with the analysis of it. It's all I can absorb, and if I feel my mind wandering, I rein it back in, depending on what's on my mind. Sometimes it's something silly like a fight you just had with someone and other times it's something horrible, like a death.

Can that ever be worked to your advantage? A lot of music is about death or life or love.

Oh, yes. Absolutely. Particularly if I know what was going on in the composer's mind, historically, at the time when he wrote the piece. In playing anything by Brahms, you can sense his frustration, his longing. It's clear as day right there in the music.

Is there a composer that you feel closest to?

I can't say that there is one. I listen to Mahler and I understand. I play Brahms and understand or, conversely, I play Tchaikovsky and I don't understand. His life was filled with turmoil and it's not really apparent in his music. The composer I feel most comfortable playing is Mozart. But, no, I can't say there's one composer. I love these people who label themselves Bach experts or Mozart experts or Rachmaninoff experts! Go figure.

If you were a critic, how would you describe your playing?

I would say that it is committed. It's always committed. No matter what town I'm in, I can't help that. Committed means that I'm not phoning it in. I never do. I think I have a talent for conveying to the audience how I feel about a piece. If I can successfully get them to understand how important it is to me, or how beautiful this particular passage is, or how intense this passage is, then they experience the piece with me as if they were playing it as well. I think that is a great talent. It's not something I can brag about. It's something I was born with. I can brag that I can play "The Bee" in less than a minute because that I worked on. But this is something—well, I'm grateful that I was born with it.

You play much of the traditional canon from the 18th and 19th centuries. Would you say that you bring anything contemporary to this music? Anything from our own time?

I think the opposite. I think the music is what is contemporary or, should we say, outside of time. When people say, "Oh, I've never heard the Mendelssohn Concerto before," I hear it as a great compliment. For me, it's as if it was just written. I would like to feel that way about it because I have to play it a lot. I certainly don't want to be bored with it, and I certainly don't want the musicians on stage to be bored with it. So for me it's like I'm living 200 years ago, or Mendelssohn is living with us today.

What is your practice regimen now?

Well, it's hard to have a daily regimen, because my schedule every day is different. But one thing I have learned is to stretch, because if you don't stretch—and I mean both with and without the instrument—you're asking for trouble.

How do you stretch with the instrument?

For instance, on the G string, where your arm has to be turned around completely and you would go from the very lowest possible note on the G string, like an A♭, all the way as far as you can with the first finger to stretch your wrist. Prior to that, I give my arms a good stretching. I always do that now, always and always before I perform, like an athlete, just to loosen up.

What comes after stretching?

Well, everybody has their scales and exercises that they do. If I have the time, I'll do them for an hour; if not, I'll do ten minutes. Scales, double-stop routines, things to stretch out the fingers, get them warmed up. Also, I play open strings for a few seconds, too—I know it sounds silly—to warm up the string and get the instrument warmed up. It's extremely unnecessary, but I do it anyway.

What's your own version of scales?

Recordings

Bella Italia: *Music of Wolf, Tchaikovsky, Lidstrom, Paganini. With various artists (EMI Classics 8243 5 56163 2 6).*

Brahms: *Concerto in D, Op. 77; Bruch: Concerto No. 1 in G Minor, Op. 26. Minnesota Orchestra, Edo de Waart, cond. (EMI CDC 4DS-49429).*

Brahms: *Sonatensatz in C Minor, Sonata No. 2 in A, Op. 100; Franck: Sonata in A. With Cecile Licad, piano (EMI CDC 4DS-49410).*

Brahms: *Horn Trio, with Cecile Licad, piano, John Cerminaro, French horn; Tchaikovsky: Piano Trio, with Cecile Licad, piano, Antonio Meneses, cello (EMI CDC 54000).*

Humoresque: *Music of Dvořák, Waxman, Porter, Gershwin, Bach, Rimsky-Korsakov, Lalo, and Wagner. London Symphony Orchestra, Andrew Litton, cond. (Nonesuch CD-79464).*

It Ain't Necessarily So: Encores. *With Sandra Rivers, piano (EMI CDC 54576).*

Mendelssohn: *Concerto in E Minor, Op. 64; Massenet: Méditation from "Thaïs"; Saint-Saëns: Havanaise, Op. 83; Introduction and Rondo Capriccioso, Op. 28. New York Chamber Symphony, Gerard Schwarz, cond. (EMI CDC 4DS-49276).*

Night and Day: *Music of Kreisler, Borodin, Brahms, Strauss, Porter. With various artists (EMI 7243 5 56481 2 9).*

Sibelius: *Concerto in D Minor, Op. 47; Chausson: Poème for Violin and Orchestra, Op. 25. London Symphony Orchestra, Michael Tilson Thomas, cond. (EMI 7 54855 2 3).*

Shostakovich: *Concerto No. 1 in A Minor, Op. 99; Barber: Concerto, Op. 14. London Symphony Orchestra, Maxim Shostakovich, cond. (EMI CDC 54314).*

Vivaldi: *The Four Seasons. Orchestra of St. Luke's, Nadja Salerno-Sonnenberg, cond. (EMI CDC 7 49767-2).*

Forthcoming in January 2000, untitled: *Gypsy music of Eastern Europe, performed with Sergio and Odair Assad, guitars (Nonesuch CD-70505).*

What I want to do is play every note on the instrument before I start practicing—sort of a wake-up call for the instrument. I play scales from the lowest to the highest point on each string. I do all kinds of variations of double-stops, and the basic three-octave scales up and down.

How do you approach a piece?

That depends on whether the piece is truly fresh or whether it's something that I've heard a lot. Once all the notes are learned, I go into an analysis of what I want to do with it musically. And then I have to change all the fingerings and bowings anyhow because now there is an idea to it and this fingering won't work. Also, I'm notorious for changing bowings and fingerings on the spot, on stage.

That's playing dangerously. Do you just suddenly see something you want to do?

Generally, I want to be as prepared as I can be, but on stage I want to be as spontaneous as possible. And, depending on my mood, I may play a passage a particular way that not only have I never played before, but never occurred to me either. I'll do it on stage and hopefully I'll do it clearly enough that I bring the conductor and the orchestra along with me. I have never played a piece the same way twice.

I'm intrigued by your statement that some pieces feel as though they were "written for you"—you cited the Sibelius. What do you mean by that?

Well, that concerto runs the gamut of emotions, from A to Z. It's also a concerto that only works—and I mean that it truly only works—when you have an incredible variety of sounds, which I do, and when you are not afraid to use them. Including, by the way, an ugly sound! Including entire passages with no vibrato! The coda of the first movement, for example, is something so wild that I can't imagine playing it safe, and yet if you want to hit all the notes there, you have to play it safe. It's not very violinistic. It's very, very awkward. But this is at least one reason why I waited to learn it—you have to ask yourself what the point is to playing that coda at a slow tempo and getting all the notes if you're not going to have people falling out of their chairs from the excitement of it. I've always been the kind of player who would take a chance on stage. Be prepared, of course, as prepared as humanly possible, but take a chance nonetheless!

If it's a chance you regularly take and you still call it a chance, one would presume then that you sometimes fail.

Oh, yes! I either succeed grandly or I fail miserably. Or, let me put it another way: people in the audience fall off their chairs one way or another.

Gil Shaham

Gil Shaham is a true cosmopolitan. The son of two Israeli scientists, he was born in America, grew up in Jerusalem, and then moved to New York City, where he still lives with his wife, violinist Adele Anthony. His discography extends from the Baroque to the contemporary, and his international reputation is well established and constantly growing. He won the Avery Fisher Prize for musical excellence in 1990.

During this 1999 interview, he displayed the same openness and natural charm in conversation that he projects in performance. Though he takes his work very seriously, a delightful sense of humor always lurks just below the surface.

Unspoiled by Success

Edith Eisler

One person's misfortune can be another's lucky break. Everybody knows stories of understudies who became famous overnight when they stepped in for an indisposed star. This happens not only in the theater but on the concert stage as well. When violinist Itzhak Perlman could not travel to London in 1989 because of an ear infection, Gil Shaham, age 18, got his big chance taking over the Bruch and Sibelius Concertos with the London Symphony Orchestra. That performance effectively started his international career, which has flourished ever since.

He travels constantly, giving recitals and appearing with the most prestigious orchestras and conductors. An exclusive Deutsche Grammophon artist, he has recorded concertos, sonatas, and solo pieces and won several Grammy nominations. I first heard him several years ago with the New York Philharmonic and was immediately captivated by his innate musicality and beautiful, expressive tone, which can glow like bronze and shimmer like gold. He revels in his dazzling, effortless, but completely unobtrusive virtuosity and radiates an infectious enjoyment of the music. Yet his early fame has not gone to his head. We spoke this past summer [1993] and it became clear that, just as he is relaxed and unassuming on stage, he is extraordinarily modest in conversation, attributing not only his first big break but also his subsequent success entirely to luck, as if superior talent and hard work had nothing to do with it.

Tell me something about your background.

My parents are both Israeli—in fact, my mother's family claims to have been in Jerusalem for nine generations! I was born in 1971, in Urbana, Illinois, where my parents were doing post-doctoral studies at the university. We all went back to Israel before I was two years old, so I have dual citizenship and can go to, say, Cuba on my Israeli passport and Syria on my American passport. That covers a wide range of travel. I grew up in Jerusalem and came to this country when I was 11, and I've lived in New York ever since.

Are your parents still in Israel?

My mother lives in New York; my father passed away four years ago, when he was still quite young. I have an older brother in San Francisco, and my sister lives in New York. She is a pianist.

I've heard you play with her.

People were always asking us to play together. You know, a brother-and-sister act—it's a gimmick, it means money, and managers and presenters like that. But for years we consciously avoided it; our parents always kept our lives separate, which I now think was very good. Finally, about two or three years ago, we decided to try teaming up in a limited way. We did a radio show in New York, and somebody from Deutsche Grammophon heard it and suggested making a record, so we looked at each other and said, "OK, why not?"

That's a Dvořák program, isn't it?

Yes, we fell in love with his music when we were teenagers. The Sonatina is very popular; the Sonata was popular during his lifetime and then fell out of fashion—it's much more elusive and harder to bring off. The Romantic Pieces, too, are very difficult, but not in a way that impresses the audience. However, I'm very fond of all these pieces.

We performed the repertoire a few times before we recorded it, and the next year we did a three-week tour together, traveling across the United States from Alaska to Florida, and it really was fun. Since then, we haven't done anything so concentrated, but we still play with each other occasionally. This summer [1999], we'll play the Mendelssohn Concerto for Violin and Piano, which is terribly difficult, in Aspen.

Isn't that where you met Dorothy DeLay? I know you studied with her at Juilliard.

Yes, I played at the Aspen Festival when I was ten and talked with Miss DeLay about coming to Juilliard the following year, because my mother was doing more post-doctoral work and my father had a sabbatical, so we were planning to come to America for a while then. I studied with Miss DeLay for about nine years, and during that time I also worked with Jens Ellermann and Hyo Kang, all wonderful teachers, and I had chamber music with Felix Galimir. So I was very lucky. But I studied in Jerusalem before that, first with Samuel Bernstein, who just passed away, then with Chaim Taub, who was concertmaster of the Israel Philharmonic for many years and is now retired. Miss DeLay is so famous that the others tend to be overlooked, and I always feel a little bad about that; I was very lucky with all my teachers.

Didn't you also play for Isaac Stern?

Yes, several times, and it was great. I remember playing the Mendelssohn and the first Prokofiev Concerto, and having some wonderful coaching on the Brahms D-Minor Sonata with Rohan de Silva, a very fine pianist with whom I've played a lot; we came away really inspired. Mr. Stern told us we needed to focus more on the pulse, the sound. In the first phrase of the Brahms, for example, he said, "This D has to hover and glow above the A."

Did he say anything about those strange swells on the eighth notes that are almost impossible to execute?

I actually asked him about that [*sings them*], and he said we were focusing too much on the swells.

Gil Shaham studied with a variety of teachers in Jerusalem and at Juilliard, though Dorothy DeLay is his most-cited mentor.

Yes, most people simply ignore them.

[*Sings again.*] I guess those eighths are neighboring tones to the preceding note, as well as passing tones to the next one—maybe the swells are there to emphasize that double function. I learned a lot from Mr. Stern, because he had so much experience playing and coaching those pieces, and with music generally, that he knew exactly how to bring out everything we had in us. To be quite honest, I was so terrified that I was literally shaking, but he was very kind and good at talking to young kids; I was a teenager at the time.

You were also still a teenager when you burst upon the concert scene, and you did it without either starting as a prodigy or winning a lot of competitions.

Yes, I was very lucky: I had a normal childhood, going to school while

What he plays

Gil Shaham has a 1699 Antonion Stradivari violin called the "Contessa Polignac" after its original owner, a French patroness of the arts who commissioned a number of violins. It spent about 150 years in a French museum, then traveled to England and Australia before coming to America. Shaham got it about ten years ago in Chicago from a wealthy businessman who loaned it to him for two years and then gave him first option on buying it.

"It's one of the last long-model Strads," he says, "longer and narrower than normal; it took me a year and a half to get used to it. I've really always felt I was a Guarneri man, because I love their deep low register, but this Strad's low range sounds so much like a Guarneri that people have asked me if it is one."

Of his bows, Shaham says, "I just got a really nice Tourte that I love and play a lot, and I also have a Pajeot." His strings are Jargar for the E and Dominant for the rest. "When I'm used to something," he explains, "I stick to it."

Jordan Doner

I was studying music, and I didn't have to take the competition route. I really think that's the worst kind of experience a musician can have. When you play a concert, it's for pleasure, the audience is there for love of the music and to enjoy itself. But at competitions or auditions, you feel everybody's out to get you. Now my wife, Adele Anthony, who is also a violinist, has taken competitions and won first prize in the Nielsen and second in the Thibaut Competition, but even though she was so successful, just going through the experience with her showed me that I wouldn't have the emotional strength to do it myself.

So instead of winning a prize, you got your start stepping in for Perlman.
I was very lucky to be ready for it; somehow the planets must have been aligned properly. I had played with the London Symphony the year before, in the Prokofiev D-Major Concerto. But when Perlman canceled, I'm sure they tried 500 other violinists before me; it was my luck that none of them could make it. So I got a call from my agency, ICM Artists—"Do you think you can hop on the Concorde and fly to London?" It was really like a dream, something out of the movies: suddenly I had this chance and I was lucky enough to be able to say "yes" with confidence, because I knew the repertoire, the Bruch and Sibelius Concertos. Here I was, a high-school kid, with the option of going to English class or to London. It was very exciting, but the time was very tight, so we had only one rehearsal the afternoon of the concert. Michael Tilson Thomas conducted and he was so supportive. Everybody was behind me, cheering for me, even people I'd never met before. It was really a fun thing to do, but right before I went on stage it suddenly hit me that people were expecting Itzhak Perlman, not me.

Didn't they know?
Well, I thought they might have missed the announcement. That's when I got a bit nervous, but it was already too late. That concert was really my big break: it got me a lot of attention from the press and lots of invitations to play. Even today, people still tell me they heard about me through that story.

How many concerts a year do you play now?
I'm not sure. This year, I think I've done about 180.

That's one every other day!
I feel very lucky to have all these opportunities to play, and when I think about it, is there any other job where people only work 180 days a year? What's more, if I play a recital, it's maybe two hours' work; if I play a concerto, it's only 40 minutes.

But you have to do a lot of work with practicing and rehearsing, not to mention the constant traveling. What's it like to be on the road so much?

Recordings

American Scenes: *Music of Gershwin, Copland, Previn, Barber. With André Previn, piano (Deutsche Grammophon 289 453 470).*

Barber: *Concerto; Korngold: Concerto, Much Ado about Nothing. London Symphony Orchestra, André Previn, cond. (DG 439 886).*

Bartók: *Concerto No. 2, Rhapsodies Nos. 1, 2. Chicago Symphony Orchestra, Pierre Boulez, cond. (DG 289 459 639).*

Bruch: *Concerto No. 1; Mendelssohn: Concerto. Philharmonia Orchestra, Giuseppe Sinopoli, cond. (DG 427 656).*

Dvořák for Two. *With Orli Shaham, piano (DG 449 820).*

Fiddler of the Opera: *Excerpts from Rossini, Mozart, Gluck, Rossini, Prokofiev, Strauss, Gershwin, and others. (DG 447 640).*

Franck: *Sonata in A Major; Saint-Saëns: Sonata, Op. 75; Ravel: Tzigane. With Gerhard Oppitz, piano (DG 429 729).*

Glazunov: *Concerto in A Minor; Kabalevsky: Concerto in C Major; Tchaikovsky: Souvenir d'un lieu cher, Valse-Scherzo. Russian National Orchestra, Mikhail Pletnev, cond. (DG 289 457 064).*

Messiaen: *Quartet for the End of Time, with Jian Wang, cello; Paul Meyer, clarinet; Myung Wha Chung, piano (forthcoming on DG).*

Paganini for Two. *With Göran Söllscher, guitar (DG 437 837).*

Paganini: *Concerto No. 1, Op. 6; Saint-Saëns: Concerto No. 3. New York Philharmonic, Giuseppe Sinopoli, cond. (DG 429 786).*

Pärt: *Fratres, Tabula Rasa, Symphony No. 3. With Adele Anthony, violin; Gothenburg Symphony, Neeme Järvi, cond. (DG 289 457 647).*

Prokofiev: *Concertos; Solo Sonata, Op. 115. London Symphony Orchestra, André Previn, cond. (DG 447 758).*

Romances: *Music of Elgar, Kreisler, Svendsen, Beethoven, Kreisler, and others. Orpheus Chamber Orchestra (DG 449 923).*

Sarasate: *Zigeunerweisen, Airs bohémiens; Wieniawski: Concertos Nos. 1, 2; Légende. London Symphony, Lawrence Foster, cond. (DG 431 815).*

Sibelius: *Concerto; Tchaikovsky: Concerto. Philharmonia Orchestra, Giuseppe Sinopoli, cond. (DG 437 540).*

Vivaldi: *The Four Seasons; Kreisler: Concerto in the Style of Vivaldi. Orpheus Chamber Orchestra (DG 439 933-2/4).*

Well, when you pack your suitcase, leave your house, get ready to go and play your concert, you feel as if you press the "pause" button on your life. And when you come back, you press the "play" button, pay the phone bill, and do the laundry, before you have to pack again a couple of days later and put your life back on "pause." I've been doing this for almost ten years now, so I think in future I'll try to press "pause" a little less and "play" a little more.

That means turning down engagements. Can one do that?
I don't know if I'll be able to do it. It's so nice to be asked to play; for a musician, that's the most important thing, isn't it? If people want me to play, how can I say no?

Do you usually stay in one place for several days?
When I started out, I tried to do that. It was very enticing to spend a few extra days in Paris and enjoy the sights. Now I try to minimize my time away from home and come back as fast as I can. My wife also travels—she does solo work and plays with some chamber groups, including the Sejong Soloists, a young 13-piece string group. One night recently, they left for Japan when I had just come back from Chicago the day before; we had two days together. It's crazy, so we've learned to get on the next plane home.

BARTÓK · VIOLIN CONCERTO NO. 2
RHAPSODIES NOS. 1 & 2
GIL SHAHAM · PIERRE BOULEZ
CHICAGO SYMPHONY ORCHESTRA

Do you have time to practice on tour?
At this point in my life, I know exactly how to make use of every minute on tour, and actually accomplish more than at home, where I can be rather at loose ends. There's a structure about catching a plane and going to a hotel. I can practice late at night with a practice mute even while I'm jet-lagged.

Shaham records exclusively on Deutsche Grammophon.

Ah yes, the jet lag—how do you handle that?
For me, it's the worst part. They say it takes one day to recover from every hour of time difference, so now I really try to plan for that. When I go to Europe, I try—I don't always succeed—to have six days off to adjust, because I know I won't be able to fall asleep and will be wide awake reading or practicing at one in the morning, and it's the same when I come back. It's funny, all the things you gradually figure out. I know I can do orchestra rehearsals in the afternoon, but not in the morning, because 10 A.M. in Europe is 4 A.M. here, and I haven't slept all night and am completely knocked out. All my friends say the same. You must sleep during the day, or you just crash. In the beginning, before I knew all this, I found myself asleep on the couch in my dressing room two minutes before I had to go on stage . . . that's no way to

be fresh for a concert. I've also learned to sleep on the plane, and when I'm awake, I read; it's about the only chance I get.

After taking a long trip, do you play several concerts in the same place?

Only when I play a concerto, because some orchestras have a subscription week. That means a rehearsal, say, on Wednesday, a dress rehearsal Thursday, concerts Thursday, Friday, Saturday, and sometimes also the following Tuesday. That's the longest time I ever get to spend in one place. For a recital, I usually come in that day, play that evening, and move on the next day.

Koichi Miura

Shaham prefers to perform a piece in public before committing it to a recording.

Do you bring your own pianist?

Yes. This season I am doing most of my concerts with Akira Eguchi, who is a wonderful pianist. We travel together, which is much nicer than traveling alone, and we can rehearse before-hand—in fact, he lives across the street from us. I've also done some concerts with Jonathan Feldman and am going to make a recording with him, and sometimes I play with my sister.

Can you choose the orchestras and conductors with whom you play?

Yes, in the sense that I could say no, but I am very lucky, because most of the time I work with people I know and get along with. The first time, it's like meeting people in any other situation: you never know how it's going to work. But I haven't had any really bad experiences.

In two rehearsals, is there even time to discuss the music?

That's a great question. I wish—and I understand it's impossible, the way the music world is set up—but I wish we could rehearse more, and not on the same day as the concert, because it drains out all the energy. And for the wind players it's even worse to play a two-hour concert after two or three hours of rehearsal.

Do you get a chance to confer with the conductor ahead of time?

Yes, they usually like to have a rehearsal with piano.

Suppose there is a real disagreement, about tempos or something like that.

Then you have to compromise. But you know, I've never met a musician from whom I couldn't learn. Even if I finally have to play at a different tempo than I would have liked, I always feel it's been a good experience and that I gained something I can grow with.

Do you choose what concerto you'll play?

I make suggestions, they make suggestions, and by the third or fourth fax we agree. Sometimes a conductor, or an orchestra, or maybe the marketing department, will invite me only on condition that I perform a certain piece; if it's one I like, and if I can prepare it properly, I'll agree to play it. But one of the good things about being a sort of freelance musician is that I can always refuse to play this concerto, or go to that place, on a given date. So I end up performing only music I enjoy playing with people I love working with. It's too good to be true—I've been very, very lucky with my life so far.

That's wonderful, but you've also worked very hard, or you wouldn't play the way you do—though I must say you make it seem as easy and enjoyable as eating an ice-cream sundae. How do you choose your repertoire?

I guess I'm very boring: I like the standard literature.

Any favorites?

That's very difficult to answer. If I were backed into a corner, I might pick, among the concertos, Mendelssohn, which Joachim called "the heart's jewel," and Brahms, Beethoven.

You also play a lot of contemporary music; how do you choose that?

I don't have any rules. I just go by what I love, what excites me and inspires me.

Have you found that you develop a special feeling for certain styles at different times in your life?

Yes, I do tend to go through phases. For two years I went through a big Bartók phase, studying all his works and trying to learn as much as I could about him and his music. The Second Concerto I've known and played since I was 13 years old, so that's been a long, loving relationship.

When you played it recently with the Philharmonic, that love came through very strongly, as it does on your recording: the way you handle those Hungarian rhythms and get inside those changing moods, and make it all seem so easy and sound so beautiful. Do you play the first concerto?

I've never performed it, though I've studied it and think it's great. Maybe that should be my next project.

When you record concertos, do you choose the pieces and the orchestra?

In the beginning, the conversations with the people at Deutsche Grammophon went something like this: "These are our ideas, we have a catalog to fill, this is what we'd like you to do." And unless it was something I really objected to, I would jump at the opportunity. Now I've been with them for ten years and I really feel I can make suggestions and speak about projects. For example, for years I wanted to record the Korngold Concerto—I think it's beautiful, masterfully written, and I love it. Well, they kept saying, "No, it's a big investment, the marketing department worries how many copies we can sell," and so on. Then maybe five or six years later, we finally recorded it, under André Previn, together with the Barber Concerto—and luckily for me, it sold well and recouped the cost. So over the years, they've grown to trust me a little more and we now have a very nice working relationship.

Do you perform a piece before you record it?

Well, again, in the beginning, I made some recordings cold, sometimes even without rehearsal, which—looking back on it now—I realize was very frustrating, because one can get much better results with enough rehearsal and some public concerts. So now I try as much as possible to insist on performing before I record. It makes all the difference in the world.

But when you record with a pianist, you can rehearse as much as necessary?

That's right. I like making music with friends; as in any other field, working with people you know and get along with is much nicer and more productive than being thrown together in a recording studio. For example, a few years ago I recorded the Sonata by André Previn, which was then brand-new. I saw the music and fell in love with it instantly— I thought it was so beautiful! André was also interested in recording it, so we did it together. Until then, I had known him only in his conductor's hat; here, he wore the pianist's and the composer's. What I love about the Sonata is that it's very much like him: his personality comes out in the music in all its sensitivity and complexity. That project was really special for me, and playing and recording with the composer was a unique experience.

Have you recorded any other contemporary music?

Yes, Arvo Pärt's *Fratres* and *Tabula rasa* with Neeme Järvi and the Gothenburg Symphony; my wife plays the other violin part in *Tabula*. Next I'm going to record Messiaen's *Quartet for the End of Time,* with Paul Meyer on clarinet, Jian Wang on cello, and Myun-Wha Chung at the piano. We'll get together in Paris for a few weeks to rehearse, and that will be very nice.

Are you adding anything to your core repertoire?

This is the first year I've ever played Bach's violin and keyboard sonatas; they are so beautiful! I've done the fourth and the third with my sister and Akira [Eguchi].

How do you build a recital program?

Again, I guess I'm very boring [*laughs*]. Sometimes you have programs with three big sonatas, which is great, but I do think it creates a sort of competition between them: which is the focus? So I really like to have one big piece, or maybe two sonatas in the first half, and shorter pieces in the second, both for my own sake and the audience's. I play pretty much the standard sonatas, and am always looking for short pieces. Do you know the pieces by Robert Fuchs? They are very beautiful. And I recently heard that there are six original violin sonatas by Scarlatti.

Do you get to play any chamber music?

Occasionally, but I really would like to do a lot more, because especially for a violinist, that's the greatest literature. Every few months I get together with a different group. I've played with members of the Boston Symphony in Tanglewood, the Israel Philharmonic, the Minnesota Orchestra, and that's really nice.

With all the summer festivals you visit, do you ever get a vacation?

Yes! After we got married [November 1998], we took a week off and went to Florida, and it was fantastic. We just sat on that beautiful beach and relaxed, and didn't do any of the things we had planned. It was very difficult to leave.

Elmar Oliveira

Elmar Oliveira, interviewed here in 1998, grew up in New York, studying first with his brother John and later at the Hartt College of Music and the Manhattan School of Music, with Ariana Bronne and then with Raphael Bronstein. His early career was studded with competition awards—he was the first and (so far) only American to win the Gold Medal at the Tchaikovsky Competition in Moscow, for example, and the first violinist to win the Avery Fisher Prize.

While he is beloved of concert audiences throughout the world, Oliveira is a true "musician's musician." Colleagues are universal in their praise for him as a soloist and ensemble player. His repertoire represents a fine balance between the central classics, overlooked works of all periods, and important contemporary compositions, many of which have been composed for him.

Man with a Mission

Timothy Pfaff

Twenty years after his stunning victory at the Tchaikovsky International Violin Competition—the first time anyone but a Russian had snagged its coveted Gold Medal—violinist Elmar Oliveira scarcely has time to remember it. Sometimes competitions work.

This one, however, hardly augured to.

"I dreaded the idea of even going to it," Oliveira recalls in the restaurant of his hotel in San Francisco, where he is making a brief, between-festivals appearance. "When I went, in 1978, it was known as a nationalistic competition. But, since I was 28, it was my last opportunity to enter. My teacher, Raphael Bronstein—a wonderful violinist, a great human being, and a man of strong Russian character—said, 'You have to go.' So I went because I owed it to him. I thought that probably nothing would come of it, but I would play the best I could. It was a very prestigious competition. Everyone—managers, record companies—went to it, and I thought, if nothing else, people would hear me play, and whatever happened, happened.

"I had very little time to prepare for the competition. And when I got to Moscow, everything was miserable. You couldn't get a hot meal. You couldn't get your laundry done, couldn't make a telephone call, couldn't get a cup of coffee. And at that time the competition officials catered to the Soviets and made it much more difficult if you were a Westerner. You were dropped at your hotel and left to fend for yourself. It was very depressing, and it was a long time—a month.

"But by the time I got to the last round, I was a favorite with the critics and the audiences. I played the [Henri] Vieuxtemps Fifth as my concerto of choice, along with the Tchaikovsky. The night before, my wife, Sandy [Sandra Robbins], and I had gone to dinner with [violinist and conductor Vladimir] Volodya Spivakov. He asked Sandy why I was playing the Vieuxtemps, and she replied, 'Because he loves it, and it's a terrific virtuoso concerto.' He said, 'Big mistake. Here no one plays it live. They study it, but they never play it in public.' When Sandy told me what he'd said, I thought, 'Those are the breaks.'

"When I played it, the audience went crazy, and even the musicians on stage were shouting bravos. After the last round, they kept us in the Moscow Conservatory for two hours while the judges deliberated. When they finally came out, they announced the winners in reverse order, starting from the 12th prize. By the time they announced the second prize, my name had not been mentioned, so I looked at Sandy and thought, 'That's it; it's all over.' When they announced the first prize and said my name, it was pretty emotional."

Still the only American to have won the Tchaikovsky Gold, Oliveira also has won other competitions, including the equally prestigious Naumberg Competition in its 50th-anniversary year, when contestants included cellists, pianists, and singers as well as violinists. Nevertheless, he says, the fruits of the Tchaikovsky were "immediate. I already had a career and was building a repertoire, but with the Tchaikovsky came much wider notice and the opportunity to play all over the world. No doubt about it, it was my entrée."

While hardly blind to the downsides and hazards of competitions, Oliveira knows firsthand their value to winning contestants. "In a day when it's extremely difficult to make a career even if you win competitions, they provide an invaluable opportunity for audiences, managers, and music professionals to hear young artists who deserve to have careers and sometimes can begin them no other way.

"And as everyone is well aware," he adds, "it's the concert reengagements, after the competitions, that really matter. Without those, any career loses steam."

That Oliveira's has only gathered momentum is directly attributable to the fact that it has been based on a commodity one rarely hears about in our promotion-crazed late century: honest musicianship. What keeps the violinist in the crosshairs of composers, conductors, promoters, presenters, record companies, and, perhaps most tellingly, his fellow musicians is consummate, versatile, unself-serving musicianship harnessed to level-headed artistic judgment and a sound work ethic. In short, musicians of all strata and callings like working with him.

"From the first time I heard Elmar, I knew I was dealing with an extraordinary instrumentalist," says Gerard Schwarz, music director of the Seattle Symphony and the New York Chamber Symphony. "The imagination and curiosity that make him such a fine musician work in tandem with a musical manner that has worn really well over time. We've been working together for some 25 years now, and we've done concertos from Vivaldi to world premieres. Through it all, Elmar continues to be one of my favorite soloists."

"My life has been dominated by the work ethic I was steeped in," Oliveira volunteers. Born into a family of Portuguese immigrants in New York, "I saw my father go to the factory at eight in the morning, come home at three for a quick lunch, and then leave to build houses until ten or so at night. He also adores the violin and violin music, and, growing up, I was surrounded by it. I didn't pick up the instrument until I was nine, and my brother, a professional violinist 11 years older than me, was my first teacher. The music was so much in my head that it was just a matter of my technique catching up with my ear. No one in my family talked about my becoming a violinist— all they ever said was, 'Good, keep trying'—and I just kept performing, winning my first competition when I was 14 and playing with the New York Philharmonic at 16. By that time it was like, what else would I be doing?"

Henry Grossman

Elmar Oliveira's career got its start when, at age nine, he began taking lessons from his older brother.

Throughout his career, Oliveira has successfully balanced orchestral appearances with recital dates and standard repertoire with more adventurous fare. Without an instant's hesitation he clarifies what he means by standard concerto fare. "The Beethoven is supreme among the violin concertos, in my opinion; then the Mozarts, and the Brahms, an absolute masterpiece. Then the Sibelius. But when I make my season offerings, I try to include concertos like the Korngold, Walton, and Glazunov among the staples, and I include at least one new, contemporary work each season. But no matter what you offer, you always seem to end up with a season of one or two contemporary works and 80 performances of the Tchaikovsky and Mendelssohn."

That disclaimer notwithstanding, in recent years Oliveira has amassed an impressive slate of premieres of works, many written expressly for him by composers including Andrzej Panufnik, Charles Wuorinen, Leonard Rosenman, Ezra Laderman, Joan Tower, and Morton Gould. He has further adjusted the balance with an increasing-

What he plays

Elmar Oliveira plays the "Lady Stretton" Giuseppe Guarneri del Gesù of 1726. "At least that's the year the label bears," the violinist says. "What I saw at the 1994 del Gesù exhibition at the Metropolitan Museum in New York made me think it might have come a bit later. The instrument is in absolutely magnificent condition and beautiful to look at. Because it's an earlier Guarneri, it has a certain elegance at slight odds with the stronger character of the later Guarneris. It has a slightly cleaner outline and a certain sculptural elegance, particularly the way the f-holes are cut.

"It's been a progression through a number of other instruments to get to this one. Along the way I've owned two Stradivaris, but the del Gesù has the character, the sound—and the power—I was looking for. It cost me the two Strads plus, to buy this instrument, and it had me in a noose, so to speak, for quite a while. But I am lucky to have been able to build up to this instrument gradually, in terms of the expense. It took me 20 years to do it, but I am fortunate enough to own my own instrument."

In 1993, Oliveira also commissioned an exact copy of the "Stretton" del Gesù from Michigan violin makers Joseph Curtin and Gregg Alf. "The copy is fantastic," he says. "It looks absolutely identical down to the last detail—including every nick, scratch, and patina change. And the sound is very similar in terms of timbre and character. I've played the copy with major orchestras and used it on recordings, and no one ever knew the difference until afterward, when I told them.

"What's remarkable about the del Gesù is the way one can mold the sound. Getting that nuance has a lot to do with playing on an instrument for a long time—it takes a certain amount of time for an instrument to develop to its peak. But at times one needs to put the original down and let it rest, and play another instrument. With such an exceptional copy, it's easier to switch from one to the other. All the measurements are exact."

Oliveira has been collecting bows throughout his career, has "a lot" of them, and switches among them. "They're all French. I started collecting Sartorys early on. The four I use most are a Sartory, a Simon, a Peccatte, and an Henry. My choice of bow depends on the character of the piece, how the bow feels in relation to the piece—and how I feel that day."

He uses a combination of strings: a Kaplan Golden Spiral E (middle gauge), a Dominant A, a Dominant Silver D—or sometimes a Pirastro Olive Silver D—and an Olive G. "I arrived at that cocktail rather quickly," he says. "When the Dominant strings first came out, I tried them, though the fashion then was to play on all gut strings. I found I couldn't play on all Dominants, because I missed a quality of warmth in the Dominant G string. It's powerful, but its beauty falls into the background. I found that when I used the Olive G, the beauty and nuance returned— and it balanced out the rest of the instrument, making the Dominant D and A more malleable."

ly busy recording schedule. He often focuses on contemporary or neglected repertoire. Most conspicuously, he scored a critical and commercial success with the Violin Concerto of the esteemed Finnish composer Einojuhani Rautavaara (b. 1928), recorded on the Ondine label with Leif Segerstam leading the Helsinki Philharmonic Orchestra.

"When Ondine asked me if I were interested in recording it, I hadn't heard it and asked them to send me the score," Oliveira recalls. "I was transfixed by the beauty of the work and quickly agreed to record it. Rautavaara was at all the rehearsals for the concerts and the recording, which followed immediately. The concerto asks for a cadenza, which turned out to be fairly spontaneous. The only direction Rautavaara gave me was, 'You've heard the piece; write what you want.' When I played what I'd come up with in the final week of practice, all he said was, 'Perfect. Do it.'" The recording has since won a Cannes Award, been selected as an "Editor's Choice" disc in *Gramophone,* and sold briskly.

Oliveira is particularly excited about his association with Artek, a new recording company in Nevada for which he serves as artistic director. His first two releases on the label are gripping renditions of under-represented works: the *Credendum for Violin and Orchestra,* "a really lovely piece" from a CD of collected works by the New York composer Nicolas Flagello (1928–1994); and, with pianist Robert Koenig, the violin sonatas of Ottorino Respighi and Ildebrando Pizzetti (1880–1968). The other strand of Oliveira's singular recording enterprise is a recently released Peter Biddulph recording called *Amati, Stradivari, and Guarneri: The Library of Congress Violins.* The CD includes Oliveira's performances on instruments from the Library's distinguished collection (established in 1935) of rare stringed instruments.

"They're all wonderful instruments," says Oliveira, "but among them the 'Ward' Stradivari and the 'Kreisler' del Gesù in particular stood out as exceptional. The problem with these projects is that you don't exactly get time to live with these instruments, to really adjust to them. I played on each of them for only about 15 minutes before we had to start recording. It's my particular good fortune that I always seem to adjust to new instruments very quickly."

That skill proved even more valuable for *The Miracle Makers,* a Bein & Fushi recording made in conjunction with the 1994 del Gesù exhibition at New York's Metropolitan Museum. The project entailed nothing short of recording on 15 of the del Gesùs and 15 comparable Stradivari instruments. "Having these rare del Gesùs in one place was a kind of miraculous event that was certain never to happen again, and it was easy to see that it offered a unique opportunity to do a recording of them in a consistent acoustic. It also would allow a direct comparison with the Strads, which were comparatively much easier to assemble on short notice. In the two days immediately after the exhibit closed, I recorded on all of them with New York pianist Nelson Padgett.

Recordings

Hugh Aitken: *Aspen Concerto. Seattle Symphony, Gerard Schwarz, cond.* (*Artek 0004*).

Amati, Stradivari & Guarneri: The Library of Congress Violins (*Biddulph LOC 97; to order, fax [44] 171 495 1428*).

J.S. Bach: *Sonatas and Partitas; Bohuslav Martinů; Madrigals for violin and viola, with Sandra Robbins, viola* (*Elan 2212*).

Samuel Barber: *Concerto for Violin and Orchestra, Op. 14. St. Louis Symphony, Leonard Slatkin, cond.* (*EMI Classics 47850*).

Brahms: *Concerto in D, Op. 77; Saint-Saëns: Concerto in B Minor, Op. 61. Seattle Symphony, Gerard Schwarz, cond.* (*Artek 0003*).

Elmar Oliveira: *Music of Brahms, Strauss, Bloch, Bartók, and others* (*Vox Box 5086*).

Nicolas Flagello: *Credendum for Violin and Orchestra. Slovak Philharmonic Orchestra, Kosice, David Amos, cond.* (*Artek 0002*).

Karel Husa: *Sonata. With David Oei, piano; Pamela Layman: Gravitation I* (*Grenadilla 1032; New World 80493*).

Joseph Joachim: *Concerto No. 2 in D, Op. 11 ("Hungarian"). London Philharmonic, Leon Botstein, cond.* (*IMP 6702092*).

Ezra Laderman: *Concerto. Louisville Orchestra, Leighton Smith, cond.* (*Louisville 004*).

Layman: *Gravitation I* (*Grenadilla 1032*).

Guillaume Lekeu: *Sonata in G. With Robert Koenig, piano* (*Biddulph 18*).

The Miracle Makers: *Music by Brahms, Paganini, Vitali, and others* (*Bein & Fushi; call [312] 663-0150*).

Ildebrando Pizzetti: *Sonata; Respighi: Sonata. With Robert Koenig, piano* (*Artek*).

Einojuhani Rautavaara: *Concerto. Helsinki Philharmonic Orchestra, Leif Segerstam, cond.* (*Ondine 881-2*).

Joan Tower: *Concerto. Louisville Orchestra, Joseph Silverstein, cond.* (*D'Note Classics 1016*).

Vivaldi: *The Four Seasons. Los Angeles Chamber Orchestra, Gerard Schwarz, cond.* (*Delos 3007*).

"The fiddles were brought in four at a time, and with each one I had no more time than to tune it up, play a scale, and start recording. I had to adjust to all kinds of things, almost instantaneously. That went on for two solid days. Then I hopped in the car and drove to Syracuse in a snowstorm to play the Brahms Concerto the following morning."

Implicit in that narrative, an all-too-familiar one for an artist of Oliveira's stature, is his remaining career goal: "Giving myself enough time to take what I've learned about the great masterpieces and get even more absorbed in them. The last few months have been particularly exciting—and demanding. For instance, in addition to my regular dates, which included learning the [Krzysztof] Penderecki Violin Concerto and performing it for the composer for the first time, I took on, at the last minute, the Joseph Achron *Concerto on Hebrew Themes,* a fantastic piece that was written for Heifetz, for a new recording project for the Milken Foundation, which has begun a 40-CD project of previously unrecorded music by Jewish composers. It involved learning the piece from scratch in three weeks and going to Germany to record it with the Berlin Radio Orchestra. It's exactly the kind of project that excites me, and that I want to take on. But now I want to do these things in ways that are less physically taxing—to make my music before I become exhausted."

Steve J. Sherman

The challenge is the greater in a time when, he thinks, the commercial aspects of promoting music have become unhealthy. "The emphasis is on promoting spectacles instead of the more intimate beauties of classical music. But for the people who really love classical music, it's the intimate side that's more important.

Oliveira's busy schedule includes overseeing his new record label, Artek.

"People in and out of the business are complaining about how bad things are, but we also have to look at the positive side. We have more great orchestras than ever, more concerts than ever, and more opportunities to listen to a greater variety of music in a wider range of venues. It's hard to imagine beginning a career now, with the new pressures young artists face. But we all have to deal with the ups and downs in our careers. As has always been true, you really have to love music deeply to commit yourself to it as a career—as an artist, a performer. If that's true, no matter what happens in your career, the deep love of your art survives. When all is said and done, the only thing that gets you through is the commitment, and the love."

Pamela Frank

Pamela Frank combines a wide range of performance activities in her international career, including solo and chamber-music concerts, and contemporary music as well as the classics. She has performed with many of the world's leading orchestras and has toured with the Detroit, Cincinnati, and Baltimore Symphonies, among others.

The daughter of noted pianists Claude Frank and Lilian Kallir, she plays chamber music with both of them, at home and in public. She also performs frequently with Peter Serkin, Yo-Yo Ma, Tabea Zimmermann, and Andy Simionescu (whom she recently married). As a champion of contemporary music, she has premiered works by such composers as Ellen Taaffe Zwilich and Aaron Jay Kernis.

In 1999 she won the Avery Fisher Prize for musical excellence, along with fellow violinists Sarah Chang and Nadja Salerno-Sonnenberg; this was the first year in which the prize has gone to women. Frank's professional accomplishments are complemented by her open, down-to-earth, and engaging manner. As she makes clear in this 1995 interview, she establishes clear priorities for herself, avoiding hype in favor of enjoying and communicating through music.

The Joy of Playing

Todd Brewster

W hen Isabella Rossellini appeared as Hungarian Countess Anna Marie Erdody in the mid-1990s motion picture *Immortal Beloved*, those in the know didn't believe for one second that the exquisite sounds coming from her fiddle were her own. As anyone who sticks around for the credits learned, Rossellini's violin "playing" was actually the work of then-27-year-old Pamela Frank. A fast-rising star on the concert circuit, the Philadelphia-based Frank was much in demand in those days, performing nearly 100 concerts in 1994 alone.

She made her debut with the New York Philharmonic in the fall of 1994, playing the Dvořák Concerto with Leonard Slatkin at the podium. The next April, she made her recital debut at Carnegie Hall in a program that included works by Brahms, Janáček, Beethoven, and the late Japanese composer Toru Takemitsu.

But even a major concert performer can get excited about participating in a major motion picture and, for Frank, *Immortal Beloved* was a blast. "I've never been involved in anything so commercial," she said then. The producers videotaped her as she recorded the movie soundtrack (along with Emanuel Ax, Yo-Yo Ma, Gidon Kremer, Murray Perahia, Georg Solti, and others) so that Rossellini, who took a few lessons herself to prepare for the role, could study the tapes and mimic Frank's playing style. And, of course, Frank got to meet the actress. "I told her I was a Lancôme cosmetics user [Rossellini has appeared in Lancôme advertisements], and when I got home there was a Federal Express package from Isabella, filled with a year's supply of makeup."

When she sat down in late 1994 to discuss her burgeoning career, Frank had more serious ideas than makeup in mind. Unlike some performers who focus exclusively on their work as soloists, Frank maintains a schedule that breaks down equally between concertos, recitals, and chamber dates. One helps the other, she says, noting that a concerto sometimes demands the intimacy of a chamber piece, while a chamber player sometimes must call upon the bolder playing style of a recitalist.

Whatever she does, Frank appears to have mastered it. Pianist Christopher O'Riley, who has performed with her on many occasions, says that playing with Frank reminds him of the sense he sometimes gets when accompanying a singer. "There is an extra dimension to her music," he says, "like text is an extra dimension to a vocal line. You feel like she is playing on many levels at once." O'Riley finds her inspiring. "Whether you are playing with her in a chamber group or merely watching from the audience as she performs a concerto, you can feel Pamela project this very contagious feeling that she is consumed totally by the joy of making music."

You grew up with two musicians as parents. How did that affect your development?

It was only an advantage, as far as I'm concerned. I was surrounded by great musicians even as a young child—and to me they were just my parents' friends.

Did you begin studying music at an early age?

Well, I asked for the violin when I was three, but they made me beg for a couple of years. So I actually started playing at five. I mean, my parents like to say that they discouraged me. But that's not true. They wanted to make sure I was really serious about it. They probably just wanted to get me to shut up after a couple of years, so they finally gave it to me, and I started studying right away with Shirley Givens, who is a children's teacher in New York. I worked on pizzicato for a long time and then I began weekly lessons.

Did you grow up playing with your parents at home?

Oh, there was sight-reading. I was constantly reading the Beethoven and Mozart sonatas with them. But we never ventured much further than that.

Now, as an adult, how do you begin learning a piece of music?

With a score. I purposely never buy a record. Because as much as people say, "Oh, I won't be influenced," you're bound to be influenced. And the score is, of course, the bible. So I spend a lot of time with the score before I even go near the instrument. I just sit and try to hear in my head what's on the written page.

You don't play it straight out?

No, but I sing it. I won't sing the whole piece. But it's a good thing to do, nonetheless, especially when you don't want to have instrumental concerns taint your view of how something should go. When you learn a piece on an instrument, instrumental concerns immediately get in the way. Singing is the purest way of learning music. The voice is the ultimate instrument.

Do you ever do any kind of extramusical research on a piece? Will you go read about the composer and see what he or she was thinking at the time?

Yes. But even beyond that, I try to put music in the context of what was going on historically. So much music was written as a reaction to what was happening politically or socioeconomically. So you just collect literature. You get to know the composer as a person, and you begin to immerse yourself in the time of the composition. What was going on then? What were people thinking and doing?

And that helps you understand what the composer was after?

Yes. It's as if you're living with the guy before you're living with his work. And it always throws you for a loop, what the people were about. For instance, I'll never forget when I was little, and I first found out that Brahms had a really high voice. Brahms! It blew my mind. You think of Brahms as this big, warm baritone—you know, full-bodied.

A big fat guy with a beard.

Exactly. Yet he had this squeaky little voice. So when you're learning a piece, it can be amusing at the very least, and often very helpful, to try

Uhat she plays

Pamela Frank has been playing a Giuseppe Guarneri del Gesù, the "ex-Wieniawski," made in Cremona in 1736 and named for Henryk Wieniawski (1835–1880), the famous Polish virtuoso. Frank has been playing the instrument since the summer of 1988, but she does not own it herself.

"It found me," she explains. "I have to tell you, I was born under a lucky star as far as this was concerned. I met, completely by chance, an instrument collector who heard me play and offered me this instrument on indefinite loan. I don't want to mention his name, because people can get harassed—but he decided that he was going to give the instrument to [the] Curtis [School of Music] on the condition that I could play on it for the rest of my life. So I take care of the insurance. It's fantastic—thank God for people like that. There are too many people in the world who hoard instruments and put them behind glass, and what for?"

Frank says she grew up playing "transient" instruments. "Shirley Givens, my teacher, had a bunch of instruments she would lend out," she remembers. "And my father's brother is an amateur violinist; for a while I played on a Klotz that I borrowed from him. I also played on a rented Czechoslovakian instrument." The only instruments she owns now are the first full-size violin she ever had, a French "no-name" (which, she says, "you can't hear past the tenth row"), and a contemporary instrument made in 1988 by Terry Borman in Utah. "You never know what's going to happen to those instruments," she points out. "They might actually develop into something great. This one is made on a Guarneri model."

When asked whether she has ever played an instrument that felt perfect for her, Frank responds with enthusiasm, "Yes. Oh, God! The first time I played with Sascha Schneider in Carnegie Hall—the Vivaldi Concerto—he called up [New York–based dealer] Jacques Français and said, 'Give her your best instrument.' So I went in and tried an instrument that Perlman had been playing on, the 'Bazzini' del Gesù. I don't know how I would react to it now, now that I have more experience with instruments. But I had never played on anything like that before. You could not take it out of my hands; they had to throw me out of the shop. I got to take it home for a week, and I just couldn't put it back in the case.

"That was in 1986. It has happened to me with one other instrument also, another del Gesù—you can tell I'm not a Strad person. I don't know the name of it, and it's privately owned. But you had to rip it out of my hands. The connection was so strong, it was like another human being. It was just an extension of the voice, with endless possibilities on top of it. Oh, instruments are so exciting!"

However, Frank doesn't go so far as to say she liked those instruments more than the one she uses now. "I think every instrument of that caliber *has its own personality to offer," she explains. "You can learn so much from these instruments. They're alive, and every one teaches you something else. I had the Bazzini for a week, while I've had the 'Wieniawski' for six years. I have a completely different relationship with it.*

"But I really have to say that I don't believe in giving people great instruments too soon," she adds. "I think you have to develop your own sound first, so you can sound like you on anything. I think that's really important; a fine instrument is just the icing on the cake."

Frank's bow is a Simon, made in the 1800s in the Vuillaume shop. "Up until a couple of years ago I was just playing on a chopstick with hair—really, a $50 bow," Frank says. "This has changed my life. The power of the bow is greatly underestimated. It doesn't change your basic sound; you should be able to get your sound, or a great sound, on any cigar box and any chopstick. But then we're talking about the last five percent—subtlety, color, gradations of shading. It's more what I notice than what anybody else would, but it really makes a difference. It's part of expanding the palette of sound."

As for strings, Frank uses Dominants, and she confesses that she rarely changes them. "I'm really bad with basic maintenance. Dominants last about two weeks, and I keep them on for half a year. I should probably pay more attention to those things. I never rehair my bow, either."

to get to know the person who wrote the so-called masterpiece that you're embarking on.

Could it ever alienate you from a piece? Suppose you don't like the guy after you read about him.

It's not about liking him; instead, it's a matter of just getting more insight into what went into a piece. A lot of composers' ideas can be misconstrued. Take Brahms again. People tend to play his music as if it were all fat and round and slow. And we think of Brahms as an old man a lot of the time. But during the time he was writing most of his works, he was young and incredibly virile. And, knowing that, it can change your preconception of what a piece should sound like. Even if a composer had a sordid past, I'd rather know about it. Because no matter what I learn, it can contribute to my playing of that person's music.

In that sense, I'm interested in the notion of musicians being like actors. They play by adopting the personality of the composer.

Yes, but there's a danger with that. I think what you're talking about is "style," in a certain way, and while I think stylistic concerns are important, they are not to be emphasized in and of themselves. I, for instance, don't subscribe to all the fuss over Baroque and other period-performance practices, because I don't think we actually know what went on. And I don't think we'll ever know. I mean, you can't play Mozart the way you play Brahms, and you can't play Brahms the way you play Mozart. However, the bottom line is that it's all just music, in a certain way. Yes, you have to be an actor. But some people take that to such an extreme that it actually eclipses the music as music.

And I suppose in the end, if you're too facile at being an actor in that sense, you lose your individual style. And then you have to ask what it is that you have brought to the music.

Exactly. It's a dangerous balance. I really believe that the musician is the middleman and can't go too far in either direction. Sometimes you get people whose personalities get so in the way that you only notice the person instead of the music. There is a great trend these days: people don't go to hear the Beethoven Violin Concerto, they go to hear so-and-so play the Beethoven Violin Concerto.

Still, it seems that there has been a real evening out of personality in concert music these days. People don't talk about performers the way that they spoke about Heifetz or Rubinstein or Callas. And that's a shame.

Well, I think all these extremes are dangerous. Yes, it's true, we do miss personality. And I actually have to blame recordings and the recording industry. It's just too easy to imitate. People buy CDs and hear a perfect performance, and then they're bound to be disappointed when they go to the concert hall. In fact, why should they go to the concert hall at all?

They could sit on their couches and listen to a perfect version of something, which is not realistic.

Do you worry about the future of live music making for that reason?

I worry less about it because of recordings, and more because of the educational system. You know, you are so struck by it when you go to European countries, where music is just one of the things that's dealt with in the home. It's a part of growing up.

There's a much more lively amateur musical community in Europe.

Oh, absolutely. We're a very young country, and we don't have a history, really, and definitely not that sense of tradition at all. So it's much more artificially created here, but it's not being created enough. I mean, if it doesn't start in the home, it's much harder to get it going in the schools. So that's the kind of thing I worry about, which is why I try to go into schools as much as I can, or even just have open discussions before concerts to make music—or the concert—seem less formal and more accessible. It's very important for somebody my age to be able to relate to other people my age, to show them that I'm relatively normal, interested in the same things they are. If I were an orchestra manager, I would have one concert a week all in blue jeans.

Speaking of that, how do you feel about the shift in the promotion of recordings, with performers getting dressed up and doing sexy covers?

I feel two ways about it. I feel like that's not the way I would go personally, because I have a more idealistic view about music. And I am not interested in publicizing myself—maybe to a fault, I don't know. But, on the other hand, I feel that maybe it has value. I have a lot of friends who are trying that sort of crossover experimentation to appeal to the masses. And they make a good argument. Maybe we can't be so selective about who we want in the concert hall. Just don't let it get in the way of the music! Yes, a concert is a visual experience, and I think it's important that the audience be able to enjoy it as a visual experience as well—otherwise they could stay home and listen to their CDs. But when you start noticing the appearance more than the music, that's a danger point. There are people who go to great extremes to look outlandish, and that, I think, can get in the way.

Let's talk a little bit about chamber music. Tell me about that mysterious thing that happens when a chamber group blends so miraculously into one sound. How does it work and what does it feel like?

There's no real formula for chamber music, except to be very open from the beginning and to do what it takes to make the other guys play their best. Which means not necessarily imposing your ideas all the time, but playing in such a way, discussing things in such a way, as to bring out the best in other people. That's really the key, I think.

But how do you figure out what brings out the best in someone else?

Well, that's where I think psychology has so much to do with it, and
that's why I find the whole thing so fascinating. If I hadn't become a violinist, I would have been a psychologist. You learn what to do by spend-
ing time with people. In most chamber-music situations, you don't meet
at the dress rehearsal. You play together a long time and you become a
part of that person's life, and it becomes very clear from the beginning
which techniques work and which don't. Fragile egos, oversensitivity,
undersensitivity, how direct you can be—all of that becomes apparent
very quickly.

Frank with Chopin Trio
partners Emanuel Ax
and Yo-Yo Ma.

*But how interesting, that in getting to know some-
one you learn not only what makes them mad or
what makes them laugh, but also what makes
them want to phrase something a certain way.*

And when it comes to that kind of telepathic
music making, there are no formulas. Either
there's a chemistry that works between people or
there isn't. Now, that kind of music making I have
with my father, which we always say is because
we're genetically programmed. I was brought up
with his standards, his priorities in music. We
tend to favor the same things and ignore the same
things. And because we know each other so well as people, we can feel
a mile away what's going to happen. So there is that, which doesn't happen to that degree very often; but where it doesn't exist, I still think you
can manufacture it.

How?

Well, you can certainly talk it through, but I think there is actually too
much importance placed on discussion. No, I think it's most helpful
just to play, play, and play, over and over. Since your playing is an extension of your personality and the other players' playing is an extension
of their personalities, it's a way of getting to know each other.

I guess so much of music making is nonintellectual.

Oh, absolutely. You know, the way Rudolf Serkin worked was to say
almost nothing. When I played with him, he hardly said anything—just
played through the piece or the movement many, many, many times.
And really, so much goes unsaid—which is, in a way, a lot stronger. You
can get a feeling for how people phrase, how people emote, whether
one note comes from something and goes to another. It all becomes
very clear. And that's why I think rehearsing verbally can sometimes get
in the way.

Is there as much freedom in performing a chamber-music piece as there is in performing a solo piece? You can certainly go more directions on your own, I would imagine, when you're performing solo.

No, I don't think so actually, though that's a logical conclusion to reach. I really think that it's all the same. That's the danger with solo playing: the soloist's mentality is such that one thinks one can just do whatever one wants. But, in fact, I would say it's less liberating. If you have a hundred people behind you, you cannot expect them to follow you. The reality of the situation is that you end up following a lot of the time yourself.

It still would seem to me that the nature of a concerto is different than the nature of a chamber piece, and that a chamber piece is executed by the composer to sound like it's one sound.

That's very true. But I think it comes down to the fact that if you're dealing with four people versus a hundred, that sense of trust that you can establish is much stronger and much more immediate. You simply can't do that with a hundred people.

And, of course, in a chamber group they're sitting right there with you. You're staring at them.

Exactly. The nature of rehearsing is different, too. And when you have that foundation, anything is possible. When you take chances or when you feel free to experiment in a concerto situation, you have to be much clearer. You have to telegraph to the people around you much more than you necessarily would in a more intimate setting. Still, once a trust has been established, one can do totally different things as the concert progresses. And when a whole orchestra responds to that, it's just such a thrill. It's absolutely incredible!

You do about a hundred concerts a year, but how many of those concerts do you come home from saying, "That was extraordinary! Everything worked."

None! Never.

Not even once or twice?

Well, first of all, the minute I think something is incredible, I'm going to be lost. That's going to be the death of me! No, every concert is a thrill on some level. I mean, I don't actually judge a concert by how well I played. In fact, that's the last thing I judge it by. It's whether I took a chance, tried something new, tried an extension of some craft that I'd been working on at home, had a particularly nice rapport with the second horn player, learned something about timing, or other issues that I'm always wrestling with. If I can simply get over one of those hurdles, that's a successful concert to me. But I don't know if I have ever walked away from a concert thinking, "Boy, did I play great!"

Recordings

Brahms: Sonatas. With Peter Serkin, piano (London/Decca 455643).

Chopin: Piano Trio. With Emanuel Ax, piano; Yo-Yo Ma, cello (Sony Classical 53112).

Dvořák: Concerto. Czech Philharmonic, Charles Mackerras, cond. (London/Decca 460316).

Hermann: Souvenirs de voyage. With David Shifrin, clarinet; Theodore Arm, violin; Walter Trampler, viola; Warren Lash, cello (Delos 3088).

Kernis: Lament and Prayer. With other works by Kernis performed by other artists (Argo 289 460 226-2).

Kernis: Still Movement with Hymn. With Paul Neubauer, viola; Carter Brey, cello; Christopher O'Riley, piano (Argo 448174-2).

Prokofiev: Oboe Quintet. With Allan Vogel, oboe; David Shifrin, clarinet; Stephen Tenenbom, viola; Edgar Meyer, double bass (Delos DE 3136).

Schubert: String Quintet, D. 956. With Felix Galimir, violin; Stephen Tenenbom, viola; Peter Wiley and J. Lichten, cellos (Sony Classical 45901).

Schubert: The "Trout" Quintet, Op. 114. With Emanuel Ax, piano; Rebecca Young, viola; Yo-Yo Ma, cello; Edgar Meyer, double bass (Sony Classical 61 964).

Does your mood affect your playing?

No. Of course, every day is a different situation. But once you go out and play, it takes care of everything. You can't walk out on stage and wear a sign saying, "I've got the flu" or "I didn't get enough sleep." And actually, if you're thinking about those things while you're playing, you're not thinking about the right things!

What literature have you not played that you're dying to play?

French music, believe it or not. I really feel like I just don't have the flavor for French music. And I'm trying to work on that in the privacy of my own home. I would never subject other people to my playing of French music! French music and Russian music.

By that you mean Debussy and Ravel. . . .

Absolutely. And Prokofiev and Tchaikovsky. I finally forced myself to play Tchaikovsky this last summer [1994].

So up to this point, if someone asked you to perform Tchaikovsky, you'd say, "Well, no, let's wait until some other time."

Yeah. But I'm in the stage of my life where I'm trying to attack my demons, bite the bullet, and just try things. So Russian music is definitely on the list. I feel more of a connection to Russian music than to French music, which is why I'd really like to explore that more.

Are you still studying?

I play for people all the time. I don't have a regular teacher, but I play for Felix Galimir, who is like the last bastion of Marlboro, all the time. I play for my colleagues. And I play for my father, who absolutely happens to be objective.

What things motivate you now? What things do you want to improve in your performance? What do you hear consistently when you play for other people that you respond to by saying, "Yeah, I've really got to work on that"?

I guess the issue of color. You can never have too much color in your playing. Getting it as vocal as possible, getting it as unviolinistic as possible. I guess it comes down to having a huge palette, increasing the size of your palette, so that, at my beck and call, at the spur of the moment, I can draw on one of a thousand expressions or shades of color. That's ultimate control, actually, to play it not the way you can, but the way you want to at any given moment.

I was just thinking that pianists are always thinking of themselves as imitating . . .

String sounds, I know.

And strings are interested in imitating vocal sounds.

Yes, but it also depends on the music. If you're playing Beethoven sonatas, it's very important for the violin to actually articulate and to emulate a piano!

What kind of music do you listen to?

Actually, I don't listen recreationally so much, believe it or not. But when I do, I listen to some jazz and I listen to a lot of choral music, things that I am not exposed to on a regular basis. I feel so emotionally connected to choral music. You just start the *St. Matthew Passion* and I'm in tears after the first few bars. And it's always nice to listen to things you can't participate in.

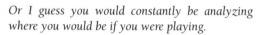

Or I guess you would constantly be analyzing where you would be if you were playing.

Right. Oh, God, you couldn't pay me enough to listen to a violin record.

Do you listen to your own recordings?

No, but I listen to tapes of concerts. I don't think I've ever listened to any of my recordings. I don't have the recording personality; I record as if I were playing the concert. So there are imperfections all over the place. I'm afraid of sounding canned, you know. And a record is so permanent; you can't change it. So I figure what I can't change, I don't want to be haunted by. But I have finally gotten up the courage to listen to tapes of concerts, and it's very helpful, as depressing as it can be. I've learned a lot from listening to tapes.

The child of pianists, Frank always had a strong interest in chamber music.

When you think about great moments in your own music making, what occurs to you?

Sascha Schneider, Alexander Schneider. When I'm thinking of why I'm doing this, when it comes down to just the pure joy of playing, all I can do is think of Sascha. Because that's what he was about. Playing with him—how do I put this?—stripped you of all unnecessary concerns. I mean, he was just about music and just about energy and just about communicating love and passion, and just basking in it and maximizing it. So it was impossible to ever get neurotic with him, or to get even slightly nervous. Whenever in the back of my head I'm slightly worried about something—making this phrase just right, or getting this sort of sound—I just think of him. And I think, "What am I worried about? This is just music; just play from your heart and play with your whole being." He was so liberating to play with.

And you knew him from a young age, I imagine.

I knew him from a very young age, and I started playing with him when I was 15. It really made an impression.

Is there any composer you would have liked to have met?

Ha! Richard Strauss. Strauss sticks out just because of his range of expression. The way things would just catapult out of him onto the page. The huge range of emotions! Such quickly changing moods, one climax after another. You have to wonder if he was actually an anal-retentive little thing, or whether he was some kind of passionate, expressive . . . I don't know. I just wonder what he was like. And Mozart, of course, I would have loved to know just because he was so scatological! The contrast between his pristine music and his totally foul character is, well, intriguing.

What about performers? Is there anyone you would have liked to have heard?

Kreisler. Fritz Kreisler and Joseph Szigeti, my two heroes. That would have been great. And I would have liked to have seen Maria Callas, just because of the strength of her personality. These were performers who combined the best of what we have been speaking about: They were faithful to the music, yet they had individuality. Szigeti and Kreisler were so vocal! When I hear them, I know why I play music. And I know why it makes me so happy.

ABOUT THE CONTRIBUTORS

Todd Brewster is an amateur pianist and freelance writer living in New York City.

Edith Eisler, *Strings'* corresponding editor from New York, is a violinist, violist, and teacher who has performed in both Europe and North America. She is a frequent contributor to several publications and a music reviewer for Amazon.com.

Timothy Pfaff is a pianist-turned-music critic who currently lives in San Francisco. He writes regularly for *Strings* and London's *Financial Times,* and during his many years in San Francisco he has also written frequently for the *San Francisco Examiner* and the *Bay Area Reporter.* His tastes include classical music, jazz, and a broad array of world music, particularly that of South Asia.

Stephanie von Buchau is the San Francisco correspondent of *Opera News,* is a music critic for the *Oakland Tribune,* and has also been published in the *London Times, New York Times, Los Angeles Times, Esquire, Opera, Music & Musicians, Stereo Review,* and *Musical America.* She contributes historical program notes to the Los Angeles Opera, the Lyric Opera of Chicago, the San Francisco Opera, the Houston Grand Opera, the Dallas Opera, and the Seattle Opera.

OTHER TITLES FROM STRING LETTER PUBLISHING

Strings Magazine

The leading periodical for string players and enthusiasts brings you global coverage of the string world through articles, interviews, reviews, transcriptions, profiles, letters, and lessons. With eight issues per year, *Strings* covers the personalities, music, news, events, instruments, and gear that matter. Each issue focuses on classical and new music while also exploring all musical genres in which string players are active.

For a free, no-risk copy of the latest issue, call (800) 827-6837 or visit www.stringsmagazine.com.

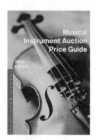

Musical Instrument Auction Price Guide, $44.95

Issued annually, illustrated with full-color plates of noteworthy instruments, the *Auction Price Guide* offers the most comprehensive information available on antique and handmade instrument and bow values. Asking and selling prices of instruments offered at the world's major auction houses are expressed in dollars, marks, pounds, and yen. A unique five-year summary by instrument and maker of high, low, and average prices shows market trends.

Commonsense Instrument Care Guide, 2nd edition, $9.95

Violin maker and dealer James N. McKean, past president of the American Federation of Violin and Bow Makers, has written the essential reference on maintaining the playability and value of violins, violas, and cellos and their bows.

ALSO IN THE STRINGS BACKSTAGE SERIES

21st-Century String Quartets, Vol. 1, $12.95 (Winter 2000)
21st-Century Violinists, Vol. 2, $12.95 (Fall 2000)

Two new collections of in-depth interviews with the world's preeminent string players give students, teachers, and music lovers many insights into the art and craft of performance. How they practice, how they work with other musicians, their performance secrets and anxieties, what moves and inspires them—all this and more come to life in this series of revealing conversations.

For more information on books from String Letter Publishing, or to place an order, please call Music Dispatch at (800) 637-2852 or (507) 454-2920, fax (507) 454-4042, or mail to Music Dispatch, PO Box 13920, Milwaukee, WI 53213. Visit String Letter Publishing on-line at www.stringletter.com.